Quick guide to

Dance Music

Ian Waugh

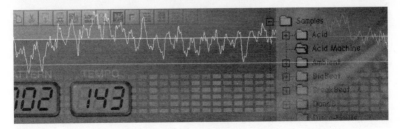

PC Publishing

PC Publishing
Export House
130 Vale Road
Tonbridge
Kent TN9 1SP
UK

Tel 01732 770893
Fax 01732 770268
email info@pc-publishing.co.uk
website http://www.pc-publishing.co.uk

First published 2000

© PC Publishing

ISBN 1 870775 69 4

British Library Cataloguing in Publication Data
A catalogue record for this book is available from the British Library

Printed in Great Britain by Martins the Printers Limited

Contents

Preface

When House evolved back in the mid-80s they said it would never last but it has continued to develop, diversify and prosper and it is now a mainstream force in the world of music. Of course, when a particular Dance genre makes it big time, you'll find bands flocking to producers wanting their music remixed in that style. And when the charts become plastered with a style, that's when the devotees head off underground again and something new emerges. So Dance music is an evolving art form and not a static one.

There are many reasons for its popularity but the most compelling one is that people like dancing to it and that's about as far back to basics as you can go! Dance also created a new type of music hero – the DJ. The traditional DJ arts of beat mixing, scratching and record manipulation were augmented by laying down new grooves from a drum machine, playing samples and adding synth lines.

And DJs proved that you don't have to be a keyboard or guitar wizard to make good music. A good ear, a deft and flexible wrist (preferably two) and a sense of rhythm and timing could just as easily be used to produce music as seven years in a music academy.

The 80s also saw the rise of sequencing and sampling technology and people discovered that you could 'construct' a piece of music as well as play it. In the 90s when computers became more powerful, the various genres of Dance were being practised by 'home' musicians and more than a few became DJs or landed a record deal.

And that's where this book comes in – to help you make Dance music with your computer. This is a new and exciting way of music production and anyone can do it although no one can guarantee that you'll become famous – musical talent still has a part to play. But this book will certainly help you get started. It looks at the major Dance genres, explains what makes them tick and shows how you can create your own Dance music on your computer using a range of software tools.

Respect.

Dedication

To Julia, my wife

...who makes my heart Dance...

With much love

Before we start, we need to run through a couple of explanations and definitions, describe what we're going to cover in the book and list some of the gear you will need.

You can use a whole mound of gear to write Dance music – if you have a bottomless pocket – but the good news is, you can do virtually everything with a computer and software, and that's the approach we look at in this book.

Before we start...

While bearing in mind the fact that you usually get what you pay for – if you're lucky! – you can start with nothing more than a computer, a sound card and freeware, shareware or inexpensive commercial software. This allows you to see which approach suits you best before spending your hard-earned on anything heavy.

You will need a working knowledge of your equipment, which could involve reading the manuals, and you'll need to know a little about MIDI and digital audio. If you're a newcomer or a little rusty, check out the book list in the Appendix.

The hardware

Virtually all Dance music is created either totally electronically or much of the production is done electronically. We're talking synthesisers, drum machines, computers, sequencers and software (yes, lots of software) rather than bands. Even though some Dance music contains vocals and uses recordings of acoustic sounds, the creation and construction process is essentially electronic.

You need a computer of course, plus a sound card. How powerful the computer needs to be depends upon the software you want to use, how many tracks you want to play and digital effects you want to use. If it's a fairly new computer it will probably be just fine but check how much RAM it has because digital audio processing is very memory-hungry. If the computer starts running out of memory it may use the hard disk as a temporary storage area which will slow everything down and possibly create clicks and glitches in the output. 64Mb ought to be regarded as the bare minimum with 128Mb a better choice. If you're using a heavyweight program or doing heavyweight things, 256Mb is not too much.

PC or Mac?
The fact is, there is lots more music software for the PC than the Mac. However, if you already have a Mac worry not 'cause you can still make Dance music, only the choice of tools is somewhat more limited.

Monitor speakers

You can use the fifteen quid jobbies which came with your computer system but you'll probably find they just don't have the bass response for Dance music. Try playing your favourite Dance CD through them and compare it with the sound you get through a hi fi. If you use small speakers to write and mix a song it will most likely sound terrible when played on another system. So invest in a decent set of speakers, maybe ones with woofers or sub-woofers.

One potential problem here is that if you have really good speakers they may show up any deficiencies in your soundcard. Can't win, can you? The major problem is likely to be with 'consumer' sound cards pre-fitted to PCs. They may be fine for games but probably cost no more than a tenner and aren't really designed for music.

Sound cards

New sound cards come out every month so if you need to upgrade your card, check the reviews in the music and computer magazines. While you're doing so, it's worth considering one which supports SoundFonts.

SoundFonts

SoundFonts are samples which load into the card and which you can play like a normal 'sound' via MIDI but you can do sample-type things such as edit them and apply effects to them.

Creative Lab's range of SoundBlaster cards pioneered SoundFonts but other cards support them, too. The good news for Mac users is that Creative has introduced a SoundFont-compatible card for the Mac, too.

Dance music is about both rhythm and sound. This book contains drum patterns you can program into a MIDI sequencer but be aware that the General MIDI drum sounds you find in most sound cards (and sound modules, too) may not be the ideal choice for Dance music (pause a while and reflect on this understatement).

Some sound sets include several drum sets, and Electro or Analogue kits might contain useful sounds, particularly for Acid, but often you will want to use sampled sounds. There's more about this in Chapter 5.

CD-R

At some point you may want to consider adding a CD writer (CD-R) if you don't have one already. Apart from being extremely useful backup devices – and you'll want to back up your music if you start to create a lot – they can be used to create audio CDs of your music which you can give away to friends, enemies and send to A&R departments.

The software

There are several approaches to creating Dance music and, depending on how you want to work and how much work you want to do, there is a range of software to do the job.

Remixers

The easiest software to work with, we lovingly call Song Construction Kits because that's what they are. They have an easy-to-use interface and give you a collection of sample loops which you assemble in different combinations. Technically they are more remixing tools than music creation tools but they're great fun, easy to use and generally very inexpensive. We look at this approach in Chapter 3.

Programs which fall into this category include Mixman's Mixman Studio, Figure 1.1, IK Multimedia's GrooveMaker, Techland's Future Beat 3D, Magix's playR Deluxe. Best Service's Media DJ Pro, and Data Becker's DJ 2000. All of these are available for the PC although some developers are porting their software to the Mac. Check out Mixman, GrooveMaker, and the Best Service software.

Software info

The software mentioned throughout the book is representative of what's available. You can find out more about all the programs mentioned from the Web – see the Appendix for details.

Figure 1.1 The Mixman Studio remixing software is available for both PC and Mac.

You can expand the potential of most programs by adding additional samples and many developers produce sample CDs

Wave and AIFF info

Wave files are the native audio file format used by Windows on the PC, AIFF is the Mac counterpart.

specifically to complement their software. You should be able to use any Wave or AIFF sample with most programs although some may not be able to change the pitch and duration unless the files have a proprietary format which keeps everything in tune and in time. Otherwise you'll need to do a spot of editing in an audio editor. On the one hand, this defeats the object of using an off-the-shelf mix machine but on the other, it takes you a step towards doing your own sample processing.

Sample sequencing

Also easy to use but with more flexibility and opportunities for creativity are sample loop sequencing programs. Sonic Foundry's Acid family has a large share of this market on the PC although many other pieces of software include sample sequencing, too, including FastTrack's Dance eJay series, Making Waves' eponymous Making Waves, Data Becker's DJ 2000, and Softkey's Pro DJ. For Mac users it's BitHeadz' Phrazer.

With this type of software, you create music tracks using sample loops. The neat thing about the Acid range, for example, is that as you add samples the program automatically adjusts their pitch and tempo to that of the song so they all play at the same tempo and at the correct pitch.

This is closer to sequencing and genuine music creation than the remixing approach of the previous programs. You can use virtually any sample and have far more control over how and when they play. We see how this works in Chapter 4.

MIDI and audio sequencing

The complete song creation process often includes both MIDI and audio recordings. There are dedicated audio-only sequencers – check out Cool Edit Pro – but most MIDI sequencers also have excellent audio arranging capabilities and, of course, allow you to combine both MIDI and audio parts in the one song should you wish to do so.

There are three major sequencers in the game – Steinberg's Cubase VST and Emagic's Logic Audio for both PC and Mac, and Cakewalk for PC only. There is more than one version of all three programs with facilities to suit different levels of user, and there are entry-level versions of all three programs, too. Some people may consider the cost of the 'pro' versions to be on the high side but given the amount of power this software offers compared to their hardware equivalent they can only be regarded as excellent value for money.

All these programs, including the entry-level versions, support both MIDI and audio tracks although if you start to get ambitious you may find the entry-level software limiting. It's worth trying the demo before buying an entry-level program although most companies have an upgrade path so you can progress fairly painlessly if you want to move on up.

There are other sequencers, of course, and companies such as Magix and Data Becker among others produce a range of software which is worth looking at. We mention these three because they are mainstream, and known and used by musicians everywhere. We look at sequencing in Chapter 5.

Audio editing

If you want to edit a sample you need an audio editor. Many of the Dance music programs and the sequencers, too, include audio editing facilities, but if you want more features then the big boys are Steinberg's WaveLab and Sonic Foundry's Sound Forge for the PC; and Bias' Peak and TC Works' Spark for the Mac.

However, we must also mention Syntrillium's Cool Edit 2000 for the PC. It's shareware, very inexpensive and a superb piece of kit. Mac users check out D-Sound Pro and Sound Sculptor II, both shareware and available from the Shareware Music Machine Web site (details in the Appendix).

Most software which handles audio also has some built-in effects. However, for the ultimate in flexibility, you want software which supports additional plug-in effects. On the PC this means DirectX plug-ins. On the Mac, there are several plug-in formats, the most popular being the Cubase VST format.

You usually need to pay money in order to get a program which supports plug-ins. However, once you have it, there are many commercial plug-ins to choose from and you'll find many more shareware and freeware plug-ins on the Net. Many Dance music programs such as those mentioned earlier include built-in effects, too.

If you want to chop up loops and put them back together again you need a program such as Steinberg's ReCycle which is available for both Mac and PC, or Button Production's Zero-X BeatCreator for the PC. We see what they do in Chapter 6 where we also offer a few tips and tricks for loop makers.

If you're worried about having to spend a year's income on gear, don't worry. Virtually all sound cards, even those which are already fitted into a computer, come with basic sequencing and audio software. Even if you don't have mega monitors, a super soundcard and the latest sequencing software, you can still make Dance music.

On the beat

A few comments about beats. All Dance music is in 4/4 time which means it has four beats to the bar. If you count the beats you'd count 1-2-3-4 and these are the main beats, the ones you groove to. Easy peasy.

There are also 'offbeats' which fit in between the main beats. Offbeats are often counted as 'and' so the count would be 1-and-2-and-3-and-4-and. You don't have to count, of course, but some people find it helps when working out rhythms. Hi hats are often placed on the offbeat. Figure 1.2 shows a four-to-the-floor kick drum with four hi hats on the offbeat.

Figure 1.2: It's not Drum & Bass, it's kick drum and hi hats with the hi hats on the offbeat.

We use the term 'kick' drum rather than 'bass' drum because it's kool, it's creeping into popular parlance among drummers and also to avoid any possible confusion between the bass drum and the melodic bass line generated by a pitched instrument.

A lot of Dance music uses breakbeats. What are they? They are a part of a song, usually one or two bars long, in which a drummer breaks down the beat he or she has been playing in order to signal a change from one section of the music to another. In the old days drummers would play a fill which usually (but not always) featured more hits which added to the complexity of the pattern. Fills usually take a song from the verse to the chorus.

So much for the technicalities. In Dance, a breakbeat is simply a rhythm which is not in the four-to-the-floor mould, that's all. Breakbeats are often rhythmically more complex and there are opportunities to create unique, exciting and individual patterns. Hopefully, all three.

Breakbeats can be programmed but they are often constructed from sampled rhythms and loops which may be dissected, reassembled and processed as we see Chapter 6. The next chapter lists several Dance music styles which use breakbeats.

Basic music niceties – not!

In the traditional world of music which extends into rock and pop and much chart material, there are 'ways of doing things' which have been around since the year dot, to do with music form, verses and chorus and that sort of stuff. For example, most popular songs follow a format which divides them in sections something like this:

Intro
Verse 1
Verse 2
Chorus
Middle 8
Chorus
Verse 4
Chorus
Repeat chorus ad infinitum
Ending or fade out

There are many variations on the theme but you probably get the picture. Most sections have eight or 16 bars. Furthermore, if you analyse the sections, they are usually made up from two- and four-bar phrases.

If you listen to a song arranged in this way you'll find you can probably anticipate where the changes are going to come. Not only do the changes 'feel' right, they are usually heralded by a drum fill, and the move from verse to chorus usually adds more percussion and the instrumental lines get busier.

Four-, eight-, and 16-bar phrases are very much part of our Western music culture and it's something virtually everyone understands (even at a subliminal level) and feels comfortable with. Dance music does not have to be constructed in this way but a lot of it is, and until you master the basic elements and feel ready to go beyond the usual music conventions, working with these phrase lengths will greatly simply the music construction process. Not only that but the vast majority of samples are in one-, two-, four- and eight-bar phrases.

Another reason for using regular phrases like these is to keep the bodies moving. If someone is jacking along to a four-bar phrase and you throw a five-bar phrase at them they might be wrong footed – not something you want to encourage in your dance floor patrons.

This doesn't mean that you have to stick to the verse/chorus sections mention earlier. In fact, Dance positively encourages experimentation and a song could easily have a dozen or more sections which flow from one to the other. If it feels good, do it!

Right, let's get movin' and groovin'...

2

What is Dance?

I f you're a Dance music aficionado, this might seem like a silly question. However, there are thousands – maybe hundreds of thousands – of people who 'know what they like', perhaps without realising exactly how diverse (or segmented) Dance music really is. Especially if they don't go to ravez, clubz or Ibiza.

In case you are an avid Dance music aficionado, you can put down the gloves because we're not going to get bogged down in the intricacies of sub-genre classification. One man's Jungle could easily be another man's Drum & Bass and you'd hear no arguments about that from this quarter.

Trawling for opinions about exactly what makes a particular style identifiable, it was amazing to find how diverse the definitions are. Well, actually not that amazing because music, particularly Dance, is an evolving art form and as soon as you try to put a team on the field, someone moves the goal posts, to coin a phrase. And that's the way it should be.

However, there are a few distinctive features which make certain types of Dance music identifiable and in this book we'll concentrate on the core elements of the major Dance genres. We're not going to argue over the minutiae and if anyone feels that a certain style should be a bit more like this or a bit less like that, then that's fine.

The creation of most types of music, and particularly Dance, involves exploration and experimentation, and often the combining of elements which may previously have been considered incompatible. If you're new to Dance, a good way to start is to master the basics of the genres you're interested in and then see where your heart, mind and feet take it.

Don't worry too much about the genre differences (apologies to any purists out there) – just concentrate on making good music and let those who wish to label it, do so.

Dance genres

It would be interesting to try to draw a family tree showing how various Dance genres have evolved and, indeed, you may find one or two in various places on the Web. However, it's difficult to say precisely where some styles came from or where they fit in the Dance music timeline, so such a tree would look more like climbing ivy than an oak. We'll simply look at the major Dance genres and offer a few, hopefully enlightening, words about any distinguishing features they may have.

The history of Dance music has been well documented both in books and in various articles on the Web so we're not going to get involved in a major history lesson here. However, 'going back to the roots' can often be helpful when you're looking for inspiration – Dance is not the first type of music to take old ideas and use them in new ways.

So here's a brief rundown of the major Dance styles. The descriptions are, to an extent, subjective. Trying to pigeonhole music is not one of man's better ideas – 'Talking about music is like dancing architecture', as Steve Martin said – but they will help make sure we're all talking about the same thing.

If you tot up all the sub-genres, sub-sub-genres, offshoots and derivative styles, there will easily be well over 100. It's tough enough simply separating the mainstream styles so someone has really had the razor blade out to slice Dance into so many segments. If you think there should be even more, take a look at: www.vagabondage.com/genres

Obviously written by a Dance devotee, this site can generate 1645 variations on Dance music sub-genre names, coming up with gems such as Ethno Hardcore, Techno Big Beat, Cosmic Breakbeat, Blunted Funk and Amyl Rave – and they're just the sensible ones!

House

House is generally acknowledged to have started in the Warehouse club in Chicago when resident DJ Frankie Knuckles mixed combinations of Disco, Europop and Soul with synthesised drum tracks, creating a simple but solid four-to-the-bar pattern which was very danceable. Devotees named the music after the club and it was later shortened to House.

The classic House rhythm is a solid four beats to the bar played at a tempo of 120–130bpm (beats per minute) although the tempo can be slightly higher. 120bpm is either the heart rate heard in the womb or the heart rate of dancers once they get going, perhaps both, although many dancers must easily pass this.

There is usually a kick drum on all four beats with a snare and/or hand clap on beats two and four. Hi hats play on the offbeat in between the kick drum beats. It can also have vocals (although they aren't essential) and a piano loop. It has simple bass lines and melodies are generally simple, too.

In the House

House music is sometimes called Chicago House, presumably to differentiate it from Seattle House or Manchester House or any of the 1001 other places which generated their own brand of House music...

Garage

Like House, Garage was also named after a club – the Paradise Garage in New York. It began in the mid 80s and was pioneered by DJ Larry Levan, evolving from Soul music or the 'Philly' sound. Garage shares similarities with House but its Disco and Soul roots are more in evidence. It relies more on melody, vocals with piano and other instrumentation. Even rhythm patterns using drums such as agogos and congas can play a melody. The tempo is between 120–130bpm.

Speedgarage

Speedgarage mixes House rhythms with slow bass lines. It's generally faster than House, harder edged, maybe a bit cleaner and you may discern some Reggae roots. Listen for vocoder and processed vocals.

Acid

The classic Acid sound uses synthesised drum beats and bass lines such as those produced by the Roland TB-303. In fact, Acid and the 303 go together like toast and butter although the Roland SH-101 often helps out. Popular synthy drum machines include the Roland TR-909. The tempo is racked up to around 140–150bpm and vocals are few.

Techno

The term 'Techno' encompasses a vast range of Dance music styles ranging from the electro-pop sounds of the 70s to the hard-edged, distorted and processed sampled sounds of Hardcore. One of its main purist characteristics is its devotion to the four-to-the-floor beat, its use of heavy sounds, repetition and electronic content. It normally runs at 125–145bpm but can go down to 115bpm or up to 160bpm. It can be minimalist and it can use vocals although they tend not be widespread and are often sampled.

Techno as he is now known (it could never be personified as female) is generally considered to have developed in Detroit in the early 80s and was a major contributor to the mass parties known as raves. To many people Rave is Techno, and to others it typifies all electronic music.

Hardcore

Hardcore is Techno raw. The tempo is around 170bpm although it can be as high as 200bpm. Distorted drums and harsh synth lines feature heavily. Listen for fast breakbeats and vocal samples. It often has a dark edge to it.

Gabber (Gabba)

An extreme form of Techno, faster than Hardcore, usually not slower than 190bpm and it can race along at 250bpm, 300bpm or even

---

The Roland effect

Back in the 80s, musical instrument manufacturer, Roland produced a handful of instruments which, over a decade later, found themselves on every Dance music producer's instrument list. They include the TB-303 Bass Line, the TR-808 and TR-909 Rhythm Composers and the SH-101 synthesiser.

Electro Techno

Just as Techno covers a wide range of styles, so its origins vary according to the style you're looking at. Some may point to electro bands of the 70s such as Kraftwerk and Tangerine Dream and while it's doubtful that they would now be labelled Techno, there can be no denying the influence they had on Techno pioneers.

faster. It's aggressive, uses lots of distortion, particularly on drums (punish that TR-909 kick) although you can distort anything you like, and it features sampled high-pitched, scathing vocals. It's the Cruella DeVille of Dance – if this doesn't scare you no living thing will...

Happy Hardcore

The happy side of Techno, running along at 160–180bpm, sometimes touching 200bpm. It majors on catchy melody lines, percussion and synth stabs, lots of major piano chords, strings and female vocals. Be happy.

IDM (Intelligent Dance Music)

An offshoot of Techno designed to be listened to, not danced to. It's more musically- than rhythm-oriented, it pays its respects to ambient and often plays at sub-100bpm tempos.

Trance

Trance is named 'cause it's supposed to put you in a trance-like mood. It's been described as danceable Ambient. It's a Techno derivative normally played around 140bpm and it usually has a four-to-the-floor beat. There is much repetition provided by arpeggiators and TB-303 bass lines. Listen for synth effects and layered sounds. The music often builds to a crescendo several times throughout a song. Many tracks devolve into a spacey ambience or floating piano-type lines at the end.

Goa Trance

Goa is similar to Trance but with more Eastern promise and psychedelia. It comes from Goa where many Trancers go to discover the meaning of life. If anyone found it they never returned to talk about it. It usually has a hard bass line and plays between 125–140bpm. Add Acid sounds and synthy wobbles, a mantra, a reference to some Eastern place names, a spoken sample from an early sci-fi film, and play for ever.

Jungle/Drum & Bass

Is it Jungle or is it Drum & Bass? The two terms are often used interchangeably although Drum & Bass is generally regarded as an offshoot of Jungle. If you have your own definition, that's fine. There are two claims to the origin of the name. One says it comes from a James Brown recording, Into the Jungle Groove. The other says it comes from the urban concrete jungle which inspired it.

Jungle

Jungle is typically created with a sampler by speeding up sampled rhythms. It has its roots in Breakbeat and uses chopped up breakbeat rhythms sometimes with a solid snare and/or kick on beats two and four. However, accents may be offbeat to create syncopated rhythms. The tempo is generally fast, between 140–160bpm, but it can be played at 180bpm and even as high as 200bpm. The bass lines have their roots in Reggae and are very rhythmical. Listen carefully and you may hear Ragga, time-stretched vocals.

Drum & Bass

Drum & Bass is generally not as busy or complex as Jungle (it's sometimes referred to as stripped-down Jungle), maybe not as fast and without the Ragga influence. It often has a strings component and the bass line is more upfront and with influences from various other genres as well as Reggae. The fast rhythms are often complemented by slow bass lines, perhaps running at half the speed of the drums.

Hard Step

If Drum & Bass in stripped-down Jungle, Hard Step is stripped down Drum & Bass, tighter and with a harder edge

Tech Step

A Jungle derivative with shades of Techno. Tech Step features dirty, distorted drums and very low bass frequencies.

Breakbeat

Breakbeat is more a category of styles than a style in its own right – but then, what isn't? Breakbeats are characterised by *not* relying on a four-to-the-floor beat and, at the least, the third beat is often syncopated. Drum patterns are constructed from sample loops and/or a TR-909 kick. If we wanted to be pernickety about it we could slot Jungle under the Breakbeak banner and show how it led to Hardcore. But we won't. It just goes to show that most musical styles had many roots.

Hip Hop

They say Hip Hop is not so much a type of music as a lifestyle. It began in 1973 when DJ Kool Herc manipulated the 'break' bits of Funk, Soul and R&B. In the late 70s rappers or MCs as they later became known, began to take an increasingly important part in the music at clubs by talking or rapping over the music while the DJ spun the discs to stretch out short rhythmic sections into longer ones. In the late 70s and early 80s Rap became mainstream and Hip Hop enjoyed a revival in the mid 80s.

Its core is the rhythm which generally has a slow, lazy feel around 90bpm, often with Soul or Funk influences. It's usually sprinkled with minimal samples and loops. Many people would say it's Rap although devotees may disagree but most Hip Hop does feature rhyming Rap lyrics over the rhythm.

Trip Hop

Running along at a slow tempo although sometimes at speeds up to 120bpm, Trip Hop has been described as Hip Hop without the rap. Slow, dubby bass lines, ambient reverb, echoes, female vocals and a smoky jazz club atmosphere. It should flow and trip you out.

Big Beat

Big Beat has borrowed from most Dance music genres. As its name suggests it's usually big on drums (big as in fat drum sounds) borrowing from Funk and Hip Hop with few vocals. However, it can include many hallmarks from other genres such as breakbeats, dub bass lines and Acid-like beeps. The tempo usually runs from 120bpm, maybe faster.

Ambient

In its purest form, Ambient music has been around for a long time although Brian Eno is regarded as the father of modern Ambient. He said that ambient music must be as ignorable as it is interesting so when you've worked out what that means you'll have a good handle on the genre.

Ambient was originally a broad term used to describe music without a beat and with no obvious rhythm, often minimalist and consisting of layers of sound – the Dance equivalent of New Age music. Now, the classification has broadened to include music slower than 80bpm intended for relaxation and for dancers to chill out to.

MC man

The MC or Master of Ceremonies was originally a person who presided over a public ceremony or formal dinner and later, entertainments introducing events and performers. The latter became known as Comperes and MC was hijacked by the clubs.

3

The remixer's art

We'll start by looking at one of the easiest and one of the most fun ways to make Dance music – remixing.

All songs are created from several layers or tracks of sounds. There'll be a drum track, a bass track, a vocal track, a piano track and so on. Mixing is the process of combining all these tracks into a final song, balancing their volumes, pan positions and applying effects such as reverb, echo, EQ and so on.

Remixing, as its name suggests, is the process of mixing the song again with the aim of producing a different sound or feel. At its most basic this could be something as simple as adding another drum track, putting, say, a four-to-the-floor beat underneath some Soul music or a piece of Jazz. In fact, this is what Frankie Knuckles did when he started the whole House music scene.

If you have access to the original recordings you can be a lot more creative. You can add tracks, remove tracks, process them, extend sections and change virtually every aspect of the song. It's not uncommon for a band to ask a famous producer or DJ to remix one of their songs to make it more 'Dancey' and suitable for clubland.

A popular wheeze is to extend a rhythm or instrumental section so the club DJ or MC can rap over it. Extended sections like this tend not to fit well into mainstream releases aimed at the chart market. Another ploy is to change or augment the drum track to make it more clubby and danceable.

The sounds play an important part in the finished product, too, and a kick drum without much bite or a bass without much oomph (apologies if the descriptions are getting too technical) might be replaced with something more appropriate or processed into a more suitable sonic state.

Using remix software

Mixing software such as Mixman and GrooveMaker, Figure 3.1, essentially give you a shed load of samples and sample loops and you decide which ones will play and when. Pressing keys on the computer keyboard triggers the samples so you can create a live mix. With most software you can record the mix for posterity and with some you can edit a mix which is considerably easier than having to do the remix again from scratch.

Remix software is great fun to use and you get a DJ feeling by making changes on the fly. Most of the samples are, of necessity, quite short, usually a bar or two in length, so some mixes can become repetitive. You should be able to import additional samples although there may be a restriction on their length but if you can

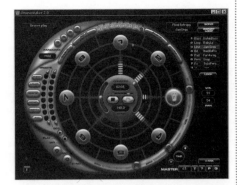

Figure 3.1: With GrooveMaker you can mix and remix loops and samples in real-time.

use samples longer than the usual bar or two, this can increase the variety of the mix.

The first thing to do, needless to say, is to play any demo files that come with the program to give you an idea of the sort of things it can do. Then experiment by creating your own mixes.

There are many ways in which samples can be combined even though you may only be dealing with 8 or 16 samples. And, in fact, the process of building a mix with remix software is essentially the same as building a song from scratch. We'll look at one of the most common ways of doing this which we call...

The ambient build

We call it the ambient build because it starts off relatively quiet and adds rhythms and instrument lines until it builds into a crescendo. Let's say we have a collection of samples in the player which fall into these categories:

Drum loop
Percussion
Bass line
Pads
Vox
FX
Arpeggios

Special FX

FX is techy shorthand for effects.
Vox is shorthand for voice or vocals.

You might construct a mix by bringing the samples in and out as follows:

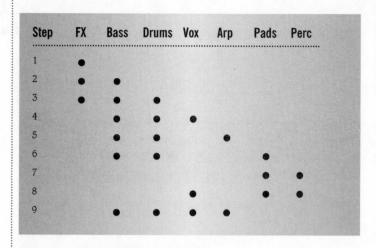

Step	FX	Bass	Drums	Vox	Arp	Pads	Perc
1	●						
2	●	●					
3	●	●	●				
4		●	●	●			
5		●	●		●		
6		●	●			●	
7						●	●
8				●		●	●
9		●	●	●	●		

This doesn't follow the verse/chorus structure we discussed in Chapter 1, rather the mix builds and develops as we go along. In step 7 the drum loop drops out as we bring in a pad and add some percussion. This could be a simple kick drum, four-to-the-floor, or it could be a riff on toms or just a simple kick and snare pattern. The object of this step is to put a little space into the music but keep the groove going. Step 8 adds the voice and then we're back in full flow with step 9.

We haven't specified a length of time for the step as this can vary according to the samples and your mood when mixing. If you made each step four bars you wouldn't go far wrong but you could just as easily make each step eight bars. And there's nothing to stop you having different bar lengths for each step. The secret, if there is one, is not to let the mix become boring, to keep the groove going.

Having said all that, if you want to use a verse/chorus format, that's fine, too.

Remixing the remix

As we mentioned earlier, a remix essentially puts together existing material in a different way. In the above example, the drum loop and bass line play an important part in the music and you can change the nature of the mix by using a different drum loop and/or bass line. Or vox or arpeggio. This is where the skill and the fun comes in – substituting one part or sample for another.

It's possible to devise many different variations of a mix using the same material. For example, solid, thudding drums will obviously give the mix a dance feel but by leaving out the drums entirely, and possibly also the bass, you could create an Ambient piece.

Another cool thing to do is to combine elements from different Dance styles, mix them up and see what happens. Try an Acid 303 bass line with a Jungle rhythm or put a Hip Hop drum loop under a Trance track. Who knows what it may sound like? But as you know, Dance has evolved by assimilating and combining all sorts of influences and many of these began by someone saying What if we try this...?

Saving a mix

All this hard mixing work will be for nothing unless you can share it with others so most software lets you save the mix for posterity. Generally, it will simply store the key movements you made to produce the mix which will create a very small file making it easy to send the mix to someone who also has the program. It may also allow you to save the mix to disk as an audio file which means you can give it to anyone and post it on the Net (more of which in Chapter 7).

But be aware that audio data can use a lot of disk space. Stereo 'CD quality' audio requires around 10Mb of disk space per minute so a few five-minute mixes would soon start chipping away at your hard disk space. Most modern computer systems come with hard disks measuring 15, 20 or 30+ megabytes in size so this shouldn't be a major problem unless you're incredibly prolific. But a CD-R is useful for backing-up your mixes.

Adding third party samples

When you have worked through the samples supplied with the remixing software – and some come with thousands so this could take a while – you may decide you'd like to add more samples to your collection.

There's a major consideration here – the samples in a mix need to play at the same tempo and in the same key. The samples which come with remixing software have been carefully created so they can be mixed and matched with each other. You may find they all run along at 130bpm, for example, and play in the key of C. Some software organises its samples into tempos and keys, which is obviously very handy. Many companies which produce remix software also produce a range of additional sample CDs so you know these will be compatible.

Many third-party sample CD producers do organise their samples

Quality

CDs are recorded at 16-bit resolution and a sample rate of 44.1kHz. This is the standard rate for computer-based audio recording although many systems can now record at rates up to 96kHz and resolutions of 24-bit and 32-bit.

by tempo and key so that's fine but do check before buying. However, if you have a sample and you don't know the key or tempo you may be in for some work.

It's not always easy to tell the pitch of a sample, even by listening to it and doing a comparison by ear although Button Production's Zero-X BeatCreator (more in Chapter 6) has a detect pitch function. Steinberg's ReCycle and BeatCreator can also help find the tempo of a loop but if you have to do this with a few hundred samples it will soon become very laborious, so you can see the benefits of buying ready-to-go samples.

Adding your own recordings

Many remix programs allow you to record your own samples. It's often suggested that you use this to record vocals. However, the record and edit functions are often rather basic and trying to lay a vocal track on top of a mix in this way is not easy.

Using it to record your own samples is also difficult unless there are facilities for trimming the inevitable periods of silence which occur at the beginning and end of a recording. And it's virtually impossible to record a loop unless you have software to help you make a loop. If this is the sort of thing you want to do you need an audio editor. We look at the process of making loops in Chapter 6.

You can do a lot with remix software but it does have its limits, one of them being the number of 'sample slots' available for mixing at any one time which is typically eight or 16. There may also be a limit on the length of a sample and there may be no facilities for programming your own drum rhythms or melodic lines.

Sample sequencing software is based on the concept of a multi-track audio sequencer but has special features designed to make it easy to work with samples and sample loops. As discussed in Chapter 3, one of the problems with working with a diverse collection of loops is that they may not all play at the same tempo or pitch.

Sample sequencing

Time stretching and pitch shifting

One of the first pieces of software to address this problem was Sonic Foundry's Acid which automatically adjusts the pitch and tempo of imported loops to match the song. This clever bit of wizardry is accomplished by two processes known as time stretching and pitch shifting, Figure 4.1. Mac users, check out Phrazer from BitHeadz which works in a similar way (contact details in the Appendix).

Digital audio samples work a little like a tape recording. If you increase the speed, the pitch increases, too. If you lower the speed, the pitch also falls. You can't change one without changing the other. This is totally useless for sample-based song construction because we need to be able to change tempo or pitch without changing the other.

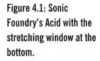

Figure 4.1: Sonic Foundry's Acid with the stretching window at the bottom.

That's where time stretching and pitch shifting come in. As its name suggests, pitch shifting can change the pitch of a sample without changing its duration. Time stretching changes the duration or tempo without changing the pitch. Acid performs these functions in the background automatically and once this obstacle is removed, you can freely mix and match samples in any way you wish.

But even if the software doesn't perform time stretching and pitch shifting (and some less expensive software doesn't), the samples provided will be in tempo and tune with each other.

Mixing on tracks

Using this type of software is similar to creating a remix in that it involves combining samples and sample loops. But here the samples are laid out on tracks so you don't have to work in real-time – yes, you sacrifice the woolly DJ hat but get to wear the producer Stetson. You also get a visual indication of the mix, and you might have more than eight or 16 tracks to work with, depending on the software. The layout also makes it easier to experiment with sample and loop placings.

Acid uses one track for each sample, unlike a true multi-tracker which can have several samples on a single track. However, the one sample/one track format makes it easy to see where the samples lie in relation to each other.

Other software, such as FastTrack's Dance eJay series, Figure 4.2, allows several samples to be placed on the same track although

Figure 4.2: Dance eJay has a drag 'n' drop approach to song creation and different samples can be placed on the same track.

it does not perform Acid's auto tempo and pitch adjustment. It will offer to change the tempo of an imported eJay sample loop if it doesn't fit the current tempo, and it has a built-in time-stretching section but the process is not automatic. Some of the eJay series has other features such as editors for creating drum, bass and melody lines.

To create a song with this type of software you either drag a sample from a list onto a track or, in the case of Acid, select a sample which automatically creates a new track for it and the sample can then be drawn onto the track at any position, Figure 4.3.

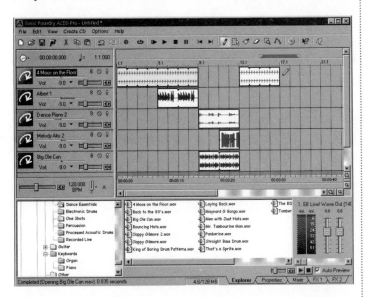

Figure 4.3: In Acid, each sample has its own track and can be 'drawn' onto the track at any position.

You must select the samples to use. It's up to you to decide how many bars they should play for, and you need to work out the song format, too. The same song construction considerations apply here as apply to doing a remix but here you have more options.

Let's look at how we might construct the intro to a song using a method we call...

The drum build-up

As its name suggests, this essentially involves building a rhythm track from individual drum parts. In fact, if you have a good rhythm loop you could create an intro like this by deconstructing it and bringing in each drum one at a time.

Let's say we have the following sample loops:

- Kick drum. A two-or four-bar pattern, this must be interesting enough to stand on its own, perhaps something like that in Figure 4.4.
- Hi hats. A rhythm which fits with the kick drum. Hats playing on the offbeat, for example, would fit the kick drum pattern above.
- Hand claps. This could be something as simple as clapping on beats two and four.
- Percussion. Having built the basic rhythm, we can now add something a little more off-the-wall, perhaps from a constructed sound rather than normal drums or percussion.

Figure 4.4: A simple two-bar kick drum pattern.

We could then assemble the parts as in Figure 4.5. The kick sample starts off and runs for eight bars, then the hi hats join in. The hand claps come in after another four bars followed by the percussion four bars later. Of course, you don't have to use a four- or eight-bar delay before bringing the parts in, use whatever fits the samples and sounds right. As it is, it takes 16 bars for the rhythm to get going. You could reduce the delays by a factor of two so it's running along in eight bars.

Figure 4.5: Assembling the parts

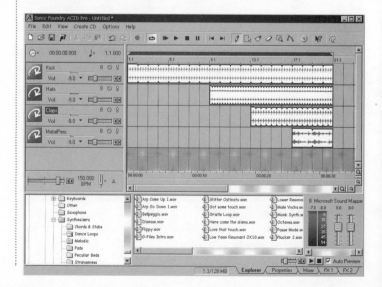

Remixing a recording

One of the neat things you can do with Acid is to put samples on top of a pre-recorded song. Although most of Acid's samples are stored in the computer's memory, it also supports disk-based tracks. These are normally used for vocal recordings or other long recordings which do not loop.

The first step is to record the song. You can play it on a hi fi and feed the output into your sound card's input and record it within Acid itself. Alternatively, you could record it in an audio editor which gives you a little more control over the process or you could rip it from an audio CD with ripper software.

Having recorded the, er, recording, load it into an Acid track. You will have to tell Acid what tempo and key it's in so it can match other samples (the manual explains how to do this) and then you can add additional drums, percussion, effects, vocals and so on. You can do a similar thing with sequencing software which we look at in the next chapter.

Another mixing trick you can do with Acid and sequencing software, too, is to record two records and mix between them, fading one up as you fade the other down. You have to match tempos but then the mixing is easy. As with other audio sequencers, Acid lets you draw volume envelopes onto the samples, Figure 4.6, so it's easy to make one fade out while the other fades in. You can be very creative here by cutting rapidly between the two recordings.

CD ripper

Many pieces of software can copy an audio track from a CD and store it onto a hard disk as a Wave file, a process colourfully known as audio ripping. Steinberg's WaveLab and Syntrillium's Cool Edit 2000 can do this and there are several rippers available on the Net for download. Be aware, however, that not all CD ROM players support audio ripping and of those that do, some do it better than others.

Legalese

Messing with commercial recordings in this way is tacitly allowed providing it is for your own listening pleasure only. If you distribute the results you could be in deep doo-doo with the record company.

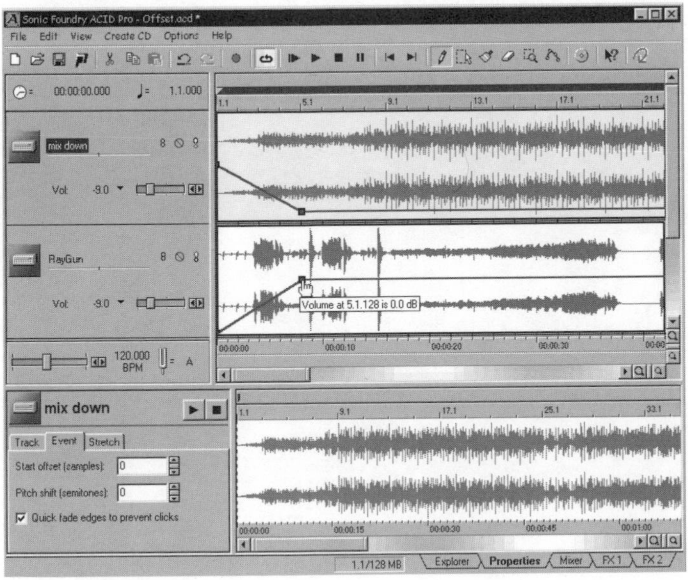

Figure 4.6: By drawing volume curves onto recordings you can mix two recordings by fading in and out between them.

Creating your own sample-based riffs

Many sample-based sequencing programs include editors where you can create drum, bass and melody lines using samples, although not all software offers all these facilities. Some members of the eJay series, for example, have only a Groove Generator Matrix – a drum editor, in other words – while others have a Hyper Generator Matrix, Figure 4.7, which is broadly similar but is used to create melody lines.

Figure 4.7: Techno eJay's Hyper Generator Matrix – or choon editor as it's known in Blyth.

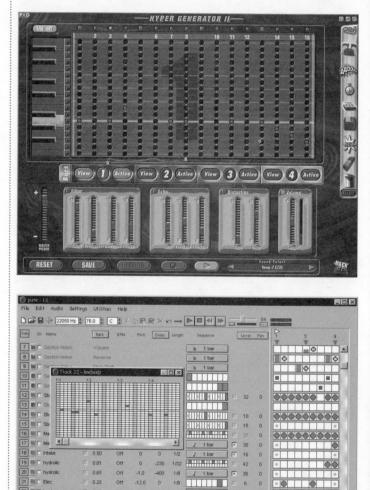

Figure 4.8: Making Waves has an on-screen drum grid and a pop-up note editor.

In Making Waves there are pattern-based drum grids on the main edit screen and a note editor for programming melodic samples, Figure 4.8.

One thing to be aware of if you use a grid for creating melodies is that in many programs there is not usually a way to create notes longer than the grid division. For example, if you were working with a grid of 1/16th notes, that's how long every single note would be. It's not a major problem with music which features short dubby bass notes and arpeggio lines but it's no good for pads or expressive phrasing.

On a roll

The piano roll editor is found in virtually all MIDI sequencing software. It's easy to use for those who don't read traditional music notation. We use it in the next chapter.

Future Beat 3D is one exception to this. It has a 'piano roll'

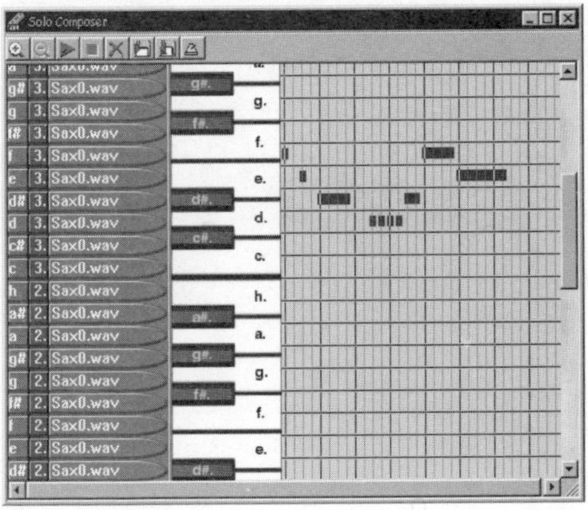

Figure 4.9: Future beat 3D has a piano roll note editor called Solo Composer.

editor called the Solo Composer for entering notes, Figure 4.9, although they only play for the length of the sample. The samples don't loop so short samples cannot generate long notes.

Programming a House drum pattern

Let's program a House drum pattern using the Dance eJay Groove Generator Matrix. You don't need eJay to program this pattern – any software with a grid-based drum editor will do the job. The important thing to note is that the grid represents one bar of music and it's divided into 16 beats. You can place any drum on any of the 16 beats.

We'll start by laying down a solid four-to-the-floor kick drum on the four main beats, reinforced by a snare on beats two and four. We add four closed hi hats on the four main beats (the same beats as the kick drum) and put open hi hats on the offbeats. The final pattern is in Figure 4.10.

We can now spice up the basic rhythm a little by adding other

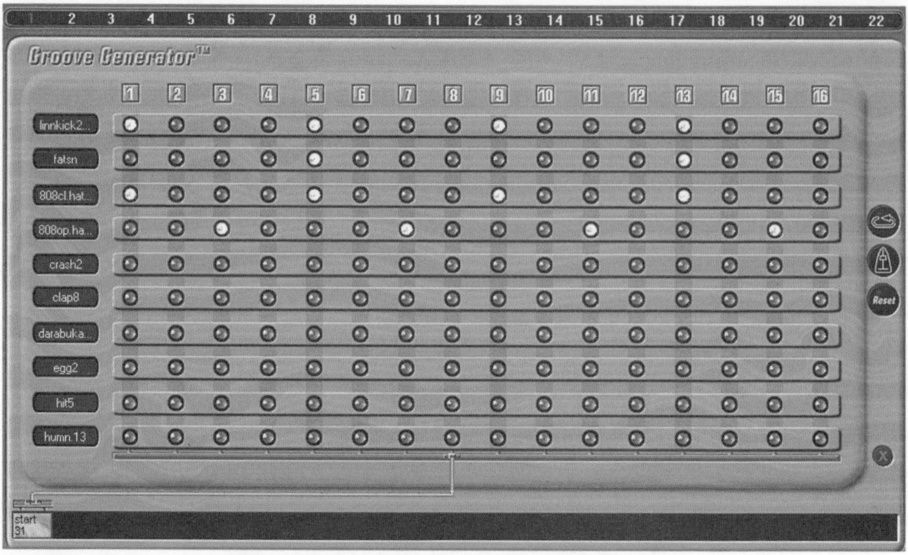

Figure 4.10: The first bar of a House drum pattern.

Figure 4.11: The second bar of our House drum pattern with added hand claps.

drums such as hand claps, toms or an electronic sound in keeping with the style of the music.

In eJay you can program several drum patterns to play throughout the song. So we move to the second grid, program the same pattern (in eJay and you can copy the pattern to save entering it again from scratch) and then experiment with another sound – here we're using hand claps.

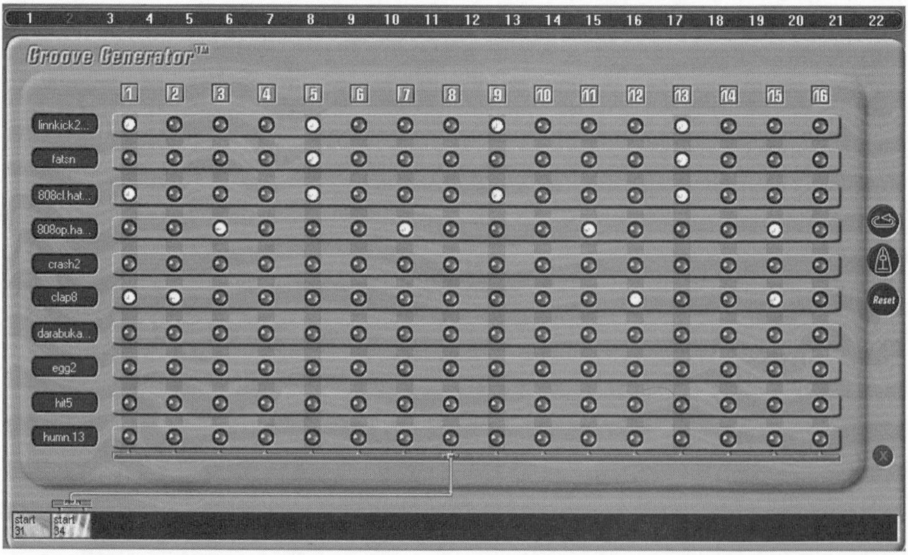

When building up a drum pattern like this the secret, if there is one, is to use the spaces in between the drums. You could place the hand claps on slots which are already occupied by drums but that would simply reinforce the existing pattern. We want to add some variety so look for interesting patterns which fit into the gaps. That's not to say that you can't use any beats which have already been used, but just use them sparingly.

Figure 4.11 shows where we've placed our hand claps. You may have created a different pattern. Now play the first bar followed by the second bar. The hand clap pattern we have here doesn't sound complete or quite rounded-off. There needs to be a hand clap on the first beat of the following bar, bar three. So create a third bar like bar one but with an additional hand clap.

That sounds better. We can now copy bars two and three and repeat the pattern a few times until we have, say, eight or 16 bars. Then we can either replace the hand claps with another pattern or vary the basic pattern a little, perhaps creating a two-bar pattern with the kick drum playing 1/16th notes on the last beat of the second bar as in Figure 4.4.

Experiment by moving some of the other drums. You don't have to move lots of drums or move them very far to dramatically alter the rhythm. As an example, put another kick drum or a snare on beat seven. That's transformed a House pattern into a Rock!

Sequence dancing

Although you can do a great deal using sample sequencing software and the techniques we looked at in the previous chapter, you can do even more with MIDI, especially when you combine it with digital audio.

Most sequencers have quite sophisticated MIDI editors where you can do things like program different volume levels for each drum hit and quantise a pattern to change its feel. (Quantisation moves notes onto the nearest division of the beat. It was originally used to correct recordings with poor timing but now it is also used to apply a rhythmic pattern or groove to a recording.) If you're using a MIDI drum set you can easily change the drums in a pattern and there is a trick or two you can do to generate different sounds which aren't so easy to do with samples (more about this near the end of this chapter).

Virtually all modern sequencers combine MIDI and digital audio recording so they can be used as an audio-only multi-track sequencer if you wish. When combined with loop-slicing software such as ReCycle and BeatCreator (discussed in the next chapter), they can change the tempo of a sample loop and allow you to change or edit individual samples within the loop.

Programming MIDI drum patterns

Let's dive in now and program some MIDI drum grooves. We're using Cubase VST's drum editor because it has a grid layout not too dissimilar to those we've seen in the sample software (if a little less colourful), and it's easy to see where each drum goes so you can program the patterns in other software. Note that in this editor, the beats are all on the lines of the grid, not in the spaces.

Couple of other things to note. All the drums are on the same track. However, if you're an inveterate tweaker you can get more control by putting each drum on its own track. In Cubase you can do this after programming the patterns. Make the track a Drum track (you should do this anyway) by clicking in the C column and selecting Drum Track from the pop up menu. Select the track then select Explode by Channel from the Structure menu and each drum will be placed on its own track.

The other thing is that, for convenience, we're using a General MIDI drum set because this is something everyone with a sound card will have. GM drums may not have the best sounds for the type of music you want to write and if you have a GS- or XG-compatible sound card or module with additional drum sets such as Electro or Analogue, it's worth experimenting with these.

General MIDI, GS and XG

General MIDI is a standard set of sounds which respond to agreed program change numbers. Program 1 is always a piano, program 17 is an organ, 74 is a flute and so on. The same applies to drum parts so the same MIDI note numbers play the same drum sounds in all GM drum sets, no matter which manufacturer developed it.

GS is Roland's extended version of the GM voice set with additional sounds and drums.

XG is Yamaha's extended version of it. Most GS and XG sound cards (and even some GM cards) and modules also have additional drum sets.

Playing samples via MIDI

You can use drum samples either in an external hardware sampler or in a software sampler running alongside your sequencer and you will need to do this to if you want good, authentic Dance drum sounds. However, external samplers are expensive and syncing to an internal sampler is not always straightforward.

By far the easiest option is to use a plug-in VST Instrument such as Steinberg's LM•4, Figure 5.1, or fxpansion's DR-005, Figure 5.2, both of which use sampled drum sounds. Although the name suggests these are for Cubase VST, the format is becoming a standard and supported by other software developers, too.

Both these modules (and probably any other similar modules which are likely to appear) let you load your own drum sounds into the drum pad slots. You can find lots of samples on the Web, on sample CDs and you can create and edit your own so you can select the exact sound of every drum that you use.

Although these modules are called Drum Modules, you can load any sample into them so you can easily incorporate all sorts of alternative sounds in your rhythm section.

Figure 5.1 (left): Steinberg's LM•4 drum module lets you play sample-based drums from within a sequencer.

Figure 5.2 (right): fxpansion's DR-005 drum module gives you control over 16 sample-based drum sounds.

Accents and velocity

Velocity essentially determines the volume of the sound, and all sequencers and most drum editors let you change the velocity of the drum notes you enter. You do not want all the notes in a drum part playing at the same volume even if you are trying to create a robotic drum pattern because it will sound very mechanical and boring.

In 4/4 time, the loudest beat is usually beat one followed by beat three and then beats two and four. On a scale of one to five the volumes might look like this:

Velocity

Technically, velocity is the speed with which a key is pressed on a MIDI keyboard. The faster and harder you press it, the greater the velocity. Velocity is virtually always linked to the volume of a sound so the greater the velocity, the louder the sound. However, it can also be used to control other aspects of a sound such as its brightness to make louder sounds brighter than quieter ones.

1-and-2-and-3-and-4

5   3   4   2

However, many types of music have the accent on the offbeat – Reggae is the prime example – in which case the accents might look like this:

1-and-2-and-3-and-4

4   5   3   4

But accents aren't fixed in stone. They contribute a lot of the feel to a pattern and you should experiment with velocity settings of your own.

Hardware drum machines – and even some software drum machines – have an accent 'drum' which isn't a drum at all, it is simply used to make certain beats louder than others. When a pattern is looping, if it was not for accents it could be difficult to tell where the first beat of a bar is.

With modern sequencers you can adjust the velocity of each note individually so you can accent individual drums or all those on a particular beat.

You must also consider hi hats when they are played in a run of eight or 16 (as they are in the Disco pattern, which we will look at a little later). If they are all the same volume they will sound very mechanical. If you're not sure where to place the accents in such a run, a useful ploy is simply to randomise their velocities. You might be able to do this en masse from within your sequencer. Otherwise simply select each in turn and add or subtract a little from its velocity value.

House drums

We'll start with a House drum pattern and to show how it's done we'll use the same pattern we used in Chapter 4. Here, however, we can show two bars at once, Figure 5.3. See how they compare.

To recreate the original we have to program bar three which is the same as the first bar but with a hand clap on the first beat. Bar four is the same as bar two. You could then loop bars three and four.

Right, let's create a new rhythm, a basic House pattern which is really nothing more than a kickin' kick drum and a hi hat on the offbeat. If you remove the other drums from the previous pattern, that's what you'll get.

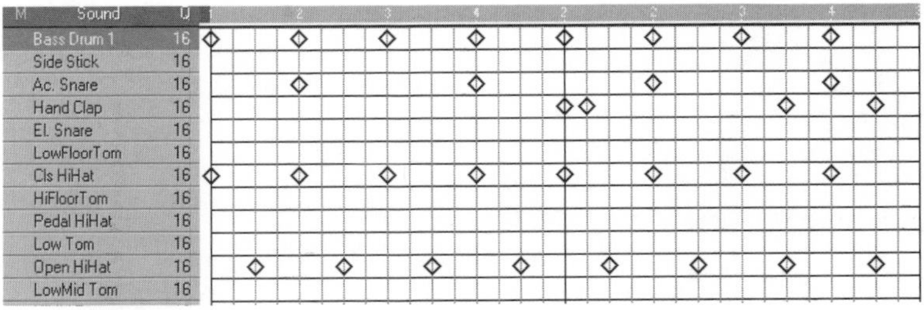

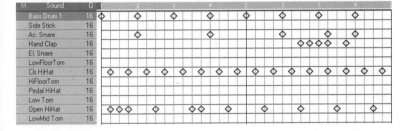

Figure 5.3: The first two bars of our original House pattern.

We can now vary the hi hat pattern using both open and closed hi hats or bring in the pedal hi hat for variety. Notice that the closed hi hat is very much off the beat which, in conjunction with the open hi hat, propels the rhythm along nicely. You will probably want to reinforce the beat by adding a snare on two and four and you can add a few hand claps to create more interest. Figure 5.4 shows the two-bar pattern.

Now, although all these parts are shown in the grid, you don't have to use them all for the entire pattern. In fact, that would be rather boring. You could run a couple of bars with just kick and

Figure 5.4: A new House pattern with hi hat and hand clap variations.

open hi hats, then add the snare for two bars, then the closed hi hats and then the hand claps. Use the straight offbeat hi hat pattern in the second bar most of the time but substitute it for the rhythm in the first bar occasionally for variation. Try creating your own hi hat and hand clap patterns. Make use of the gaps in the pattern when you add new hits.

We now need a pattern to take us from one section of the music to another, say from the verse to the chorus. We can break the beat down, build it up or create a fill which could be a totally different pattern. We'll skip the fill and look at the other two options.

You can build up the pattern by adding more drums to drive the rhythm into the next section. But don't go overboard. You break it down by removing hits. The first bar in Figure 5.5 contains a build up and the second a break down. Use one or the other, not one after the other. Although if you think it sounds okay, it's your call...

We've made the first bar more complex by adding a fairly busy

House rules

As a rule of thumb, create patterns which are two or four bars long as they make nice little phrases which can be used in many places throughout a song. Avoid odd numbers of bars as they tend to disturb the flow of the music.

31

Figure 5.5: Two rhythms to move the song from one section to another.

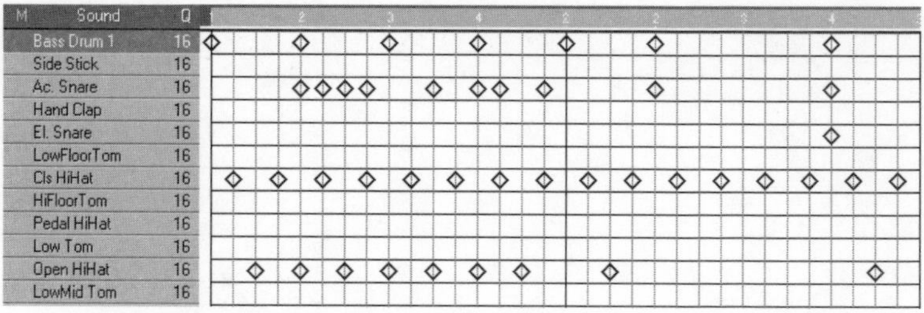

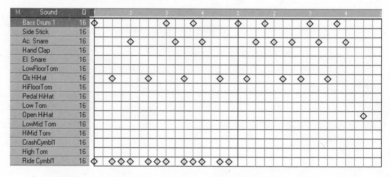

snare pattern and we've broken down the second bar simply by removing most of the third beat but notice the additional snare on the last beat to make it thwack!

Mr Funk

Some House roots can be traced back to Funk so Figure 5.6 contains two funky patterns you can experiment with. The first bar is a funk rhythm with the ride cymbal carrying the rhythmic pattern. Try playing this line on different drums.

Figure 5.6: A couple of funk patterns to play with.

The second bar is ostensibly a funk fill but it could be used as a pattern in its own right, perhaps replacing the open hi hat with a closed hi hat. Try speeding this up, too.

House bass

There's more than one style of House bass. There's the smooth style which is similar to a walking bass and there's a funky bass which jacks about all over the place.

We'll use a piano roll editor which shows the notes against a piano keyboard and has a grid to show their durations.

You can program the bass lines into your sequencer editor by clicking the notes onto the grid. We also show the lines in traditional notation so you can record them. Figure 5.7 shows a typical walking bass pattern. Note that there are a lot of semitone movements.

Walking bass

As its name suggests, a walking bass walks with a steady rhythm making few large jumps between notes; it's often simply a run of 1/8th notes.

32

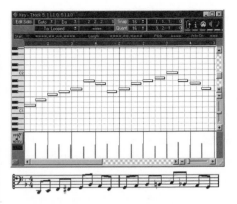

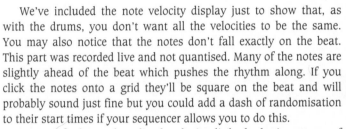

Figure 5.7 (left): A walking bass House bass line, and Figure 5.8 (right): A funked-up octave bass line.

We've included the note velocity display just to show that, as with the drums, you don't want all the velocities to be the same. You may also notice that the notes don't fall exactly on the beat. This part was recorded live and not quantised. Many of the notes are slightly ahead of the beat which pushes the rhythm along. If you click the notes onto a grid they'll be square on the beat and will probably sound just fine but you could add a dash of randomisation to their start times if your sequencer allows you to do this.

You can funk-up a bass line by playing little rhythmic patterns of a 1/16th note followed by an 1/8th note. Octaves sound good in some music and Figure 5.8 shows a funked-up octave bass line.

You can apply similar rhythm patterns to a walking bass and other unfunky lines. You may need to add more notes which you can pick from those already in the music. Figure 5.9 is a funky version of the walking bass line in Figure 5.7.

The two funky parts have been quantised to achieve the correct rhythm but you need not quantise them so tightly. A partial

Fine tuning

You can add more impetus by moving the bass notes so they play slightly before the drum part. But don't overdo this or it will simply sound out of time. You could just move the main notes which are the ones where the emphasis naturally falls. If you play the line you'll be able to hear them – they are notes two, four, six and eight. You can also change the feel by accenting different notes.

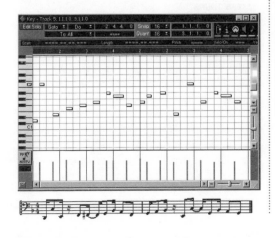

Figure 5.9: A funky version of the walking bass line.

quantise function will tighten the groove but still leave a few dregs of human feeling there, too. If you enter the parts by clicking them onto the grid, don't make them all the same velocity.

Disco beat

As House also has roots in Disco, here are a couple of back-to-yer-roots Disco patterns, Figure 5.10, which you can borrow from and adapt. The first bar is Disco 8s, the second is Disco 16s. The main pattern is carried by the kick, the snare and the hi hats. The hand claps and conga are fillers which you can throw in when the going gets boring and/or play on different drums.

Figure 5.10:
Disco patterns

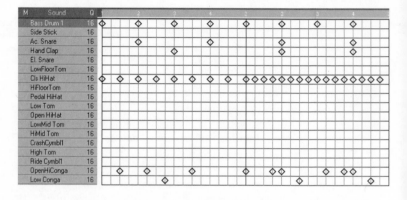

The emphasis in Disco is on the second and fourth beats so adjust the velocities of the drums there accordingly. And watch the velocities of the hi hats; give them some variety. And Disco just happens to be well embedded in the roots of Garage...

Garage drums

The House patterns should have served as an example of how to program drums and bass lines so we'll press on now with fewer interruptions. The basic Garage drum pattern is remarkably similar to the basic House pattern – a four-to-the-floor kick with snares on beats two and four and a hi hat on the offbeats – only with Garage it's more likely to be a closed hi hat than an open one.

Figure 5.11 is one such example. You can see the basic kick, snare and hat pattern, and both bars have simple bongo lines on top. These are two separate bars, not necessarily intended to play one after the other. We've brought the bongos into the drum map from lower down the list so we can see all the drums at once.

You can move some of the basic drums around in Garage if you're careful not to spoil the 'Disco' feel. Try moving a kick, snare

---

Garage drums

One feature of Garage is that the drums are often very melodic and play little tunes so you often find congas, agogos, bongos and other melodic drums darting in and out between the kick and snare.

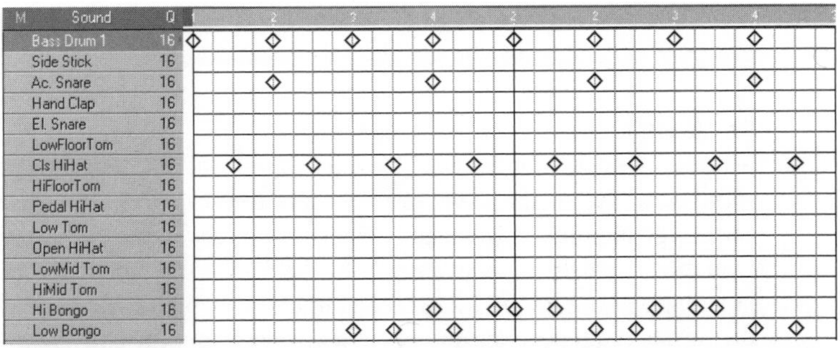

Figure 5.11: The basic four-to-the-floor Garage pattern with two melodic bongo lines on top.

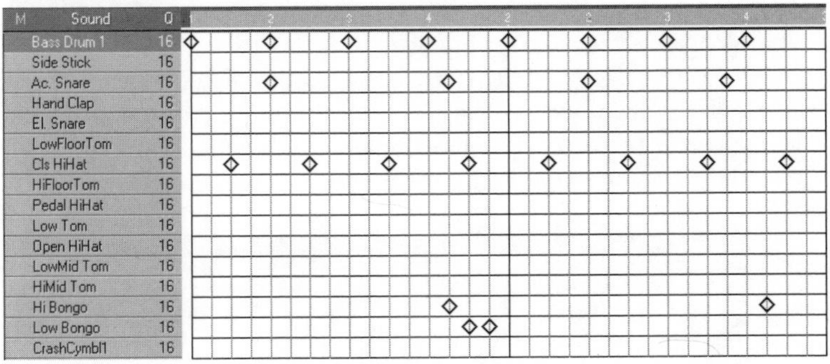

M	Sound	Q
	Bass Drum 1	16
	Side Stick	16
	Ac. Snare	16
	Hand Clap	16
	El. Snare	16
	LowFloorTom	16
	Cls HiHat	16
	HiFloorTom	16
	Pedal HiHat	16
	Low Tom	16
	Open HiHat	16
	LowMid Tom	16
	HiMid Tom	16
	Hi Bongo	16
	Low Bongo	16

Figure 5.12: Two Garage pattern with shuffled snares.

M	Sound	Q
	Bass Drum 1	16
	Side Stick	16
	Ac. Snare	16
	Hand Clap	16
	El. Snare	16
	LowFloorTom	16
	Cls HiHat	16
	HiFloorTom	16
	Pedal HiHat	16
	Low Tom	16
	Open HiHat	16
	LowMid Tom	16
	HiMid Tom	16
	Hi Bongo	16
	Low Bongo	16
	CrashCymbl1	16

or hi hat 1/16th backwards or forwards. Figure 5.12 is another two bars of Garage. In the first one we've moved the second snare 1/16th past the fourth beat and in the second bar we've moved it the other way. Try moving the other drums including the kick. We've also added two little bongo toppings. Try these patterns on other drums such as toms or agogos.

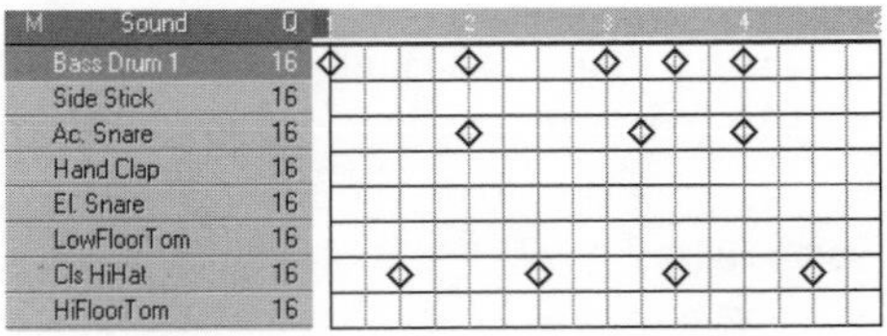

Figure 5.13: A classic Garage rhythm.

M	Sound	Q
	Bass Drum 1	16
	Side Stick	16
	Ac. Snare	16
	Hand Clap	16
	El. Snare	16
	LowFloorTom	16
	Cls HiHat	16
	HiFloorTom	16

Finally, Figure 5.13 has a classic Garage feel. In particular, notice the interplay between the kick and snare in the third beat, the chug-a-dum. This rhythm could be played on other drums or could even be a rhythmic sample.

Garage bass

With its roots in Disco, it's hardly surprising that Garage makes much use of the octave bass line which has populated so many Disco records. However, it is usually funked-up a little. The funked-

Octave bass lines

The octave bass line is not new and features prominently in Beethoven's Sonata Pathetique which was published in 1799. And he probably wasn't the first exponent.

up octave bass line we programmed in Figure 5.7 is typical Garage and the rhythm can also be used for the classic Garage piano...

Garage piano

Because Garage is so melodic, the bass line invariably follows the chord sequence of the song so you really need to work out some chords before doing the bass. There are many common chord sequences used in popular music. In the key of Dm (the key the other bass examples are in), a common pop sequence would include the chords Dm, F, G, Gm, Am, Bb, and C. They aren't the only chords you can use, of course, but various combinations of them move along nicely to a Garage groove.

Let's create a short phrase based on the chord sequence of Dm, Am, Gm and C, each playing for one bar and using the funky rhythm, Figure 5.14. It has been quantised to 1/16th notes as you can see in the piano roll editor. Each bar has exactly the same rhythm.

Figure 5.14: A Garage piano line.

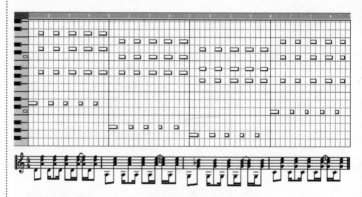

The notation has actually been transposed up an octave to make it easier to read although it sounds quite good at this pitch, too.

Garage bass 2

If we remove the upper chord notes to leave just the bass notes, Figure 5.15, we have the essence of the funk rhythm which would sound good played on a synthy bass. Again the notation has been

Figure 5.15: The essence of a funky Garage bass line.

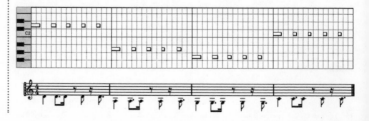

transposed upwards so it's easier to read. In practice you'd want to play it a few octaves lower.

Garage strings

All good Garage has strings so to finish off the phrase, add some strings an octave above the piano part. You can pick the chords up from Figure 5.14 but instead of playing a rhythm, just hold the chord for the full bar, Figure 5.16.

Figure 5.16: A couple of alternative string parts for our Garage rhythm.

The top notes of the chords may follow the top notes of the piano chords as in the top example, or you could play a counter-line as in the second example. The third chord here is actually Bb rather than Gm but the top F note fits the upward progression of the top line and fits in fine with the Gm chord.

Techno drums

The kick drum plays a major part in getting a good Techno sound and sampled drums work better than GM sounds. Techno can be as simple as a four-to-the-floor kick and, in fact, that's a good place to start. You can build up a pattern by adding hi hats on the offbeats and snare on beats two and four. Yes, it's identical to the basic Garage rhythm but the drums sound very different.

We can beef up the kick a little by adding another hit on the offbeat after beat four. This is a popular Techno kick drum 'variation' and shown in the second bar of Figure 5.17. In some parts of the song, maybe the very start or a middle break, you can even double up the kick drum so it plays on every 1/8th note.

The first bar in Figure 5.17 has the four-to-the-floor kick drum. The two bars here should be played with a snare on beats two and four and hi hats on the offbeat – as in our Garage pattern.

Techno tip

If you have to use a GM drum set, double up the kick drum with a low tom to give it a bit of oomph.

Figure 5.17: Techno variations.

M	Sound	Q									
	Bass Drum 1	16	◇	◇	◇	◇	◇	◇	◇	◇ ◇	
	Side Stick	16									
	Ac. Snare	16		◇		◇		◇		◇	
	Hand Clap	16	◇◇		◇◇						
	El. Snare	16									
	LowFloorTom	16		◇		◇ ◇					
	Cls HiHat	16	◇	◇◇◇	◇◇◇◇◇◇◇	◇	◇◇	◇	◇◇	◇◇	
	HiFloorTom	16									
	Pedal HiHat	16									
	Low Tom	16									
	Open HiHat	16				◇	◇	◇	◇		
	LowMid Tom	16									

Noisy snare

Techno has much of its roots in the Electro music of the 70s and a lot of the sounds are electronic and processed. One Electro Techno trick is to use a burst of white noise instead of the snare drum.

We've hijacked the hi hat lines here to illustrate more rhythmic variations, the second bar using both open and closed hi hats. Think of these parts as rhythmic additions. They don't have to be played on hi hats and, again, sampled and electronic sounds are good. Bar one also has a pattern made up from hand claps and the lo tom. Again, other sounds could be used.

These individual drum patterns aren't designed to be played all at once. Try them one at a time on top of the kick and snare pattern. You can mix and match them and use different lines for different sections of the song.

One of the great features of Techno drums – and you'll find this in other Dance patterns, too – is the snare roll. This is typically two bars long (but you could make it longer) and builds into a crescendo at which point everyone on the dance floor jumps up in the air.

It's easy to program – it's just two bars of 1/8th note snares – but you need to increase the velocity gradually over the duration for the roll. The easiest way to do this is with a graphic editor where you can draw in the velocity curve, Figure 5.18.

Figure 5.18: Creating a snare roll crescendo in a graphic editor.

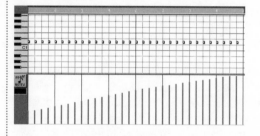

Other things to try here – if you're using a standard GM drum kit, try both acoustic and electronic snare or other combinations of drums. Certain kick drums roll well, too. If the tempo is not too fast (and Techno's bpm normally starts in the late 120s) try 1/16th notes. It might fit some music but, on the other hand, it might just sound like a machine gun! You might also like to experiment with the timing. Drawing in the notes produces a very mechanical roll so small adjustments to the timing might produce a better roll.

Techno bass

With a Techno bass you strive for a cross between funky grooviness and electronic robotica. We can, once again, draft in our funky bass line from the House section. However, instead of playing octaves, we'll play the rhythm on just one note, Figure 5.19.

There are several variations we can create on this rhythm such as the example in Figure 5.20. Again, this has been transposed up and octave so it's easier to read.

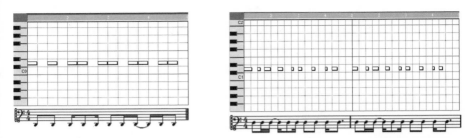

Figure 5.19 (left): A funky Techno bass line.

Figure 5.20 (right): An alternative Techno bass line.

Add another note or two and we can create other rhythmic variations as in Figure 5.21, also transposed an octave. You don't have to play the notes which are shown here, you can take the rhythms and put your own notes to them.

Figure 5.21: More Techno bass variations.

Notice the last one which is an example of the bubbling Techno bass line. This can be very effective, especially in a minor key. The accents here are important and the notes which are not the main note (not D in this case) should stand out with the main note bubbling underneath. Finally, don't discount a straight four-to-the-bar bass. Sometimes the simplest is the best.

Trance

The roots of Trance intertwine deeply with Techno and you can use most Techno drum patterns for Trance. Again, the basic pattern is a four-to-the-floor kick, offbeat hi hats and a snare or maybe a hand clap on beats two and four. All of these don't have to be happening at the same time and you can mix and match them as you will.

Much of the essence of Trance comes from the bass line or lead line which is usually quite simple yet (hopefully) interesting, and here Trance borrows much from the Electro music pioneers who might have had as few as eight notes on an analogue sequencer with which to construct a catchy music line.

If the tempo is rocking along, an effective bass line can be created simply by playing single notes on the offbeat, where the open hi hats sit in our original House pattern in Figure 5.3. Figure 5.22 illustrates some simple lines which could be used for both bass and lead lines.

39

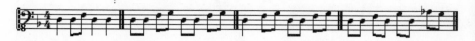

Figure 5.22: Simple lines for Trance.

One very neat trick to do with these simple lines is to run them through a filter so the tone of the line changes as it plays. So although the same line repeats, the filter sweep effect adds variety to the sound. Whether or not you can sweep the filter in real-time depends on your sound card or MIDI module.

You can draw sweeps into a sequencer using its controller editor but by far the easiest way is to use an external controller such as Keyfax's PhatBoy MIDI Controller (for contact details see the Appendix). This lets you control not only the filter but other parameters such as reverb, chorus, pan and volume, all of which can be recorded into a sequencer. The real-time control also makes it easier to respond to the music than trying to gauge where the sweep should come by looking at the MIDI data.

Hip Hop

Like most Dance styles, Hip Hop has many roots. In it you'll find references to Disco, Funk and, indeed, the Soul and R&B side of pop.

Hip Hop drums

If there is a typical Hip Hop rhythm it's funky and laid back with rhythmic interplay between the kick and snare. The next few drum patterns are really designed to be mixed and matched.

Start by looking at the kick, snare and hi hat in the first bar in Figure 5.23. The kick is ever so slightly funked-up but otherwise this is a pretty straightforward rhythm. In bar two the kick is doing more funky stuff.

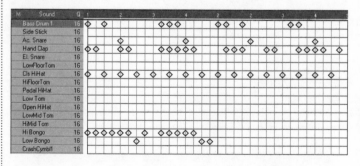

Figure 5.23: A basic Hip Hop rhythm with hand clap and bongo fills.

The two sets of hand claps are not designed to be used in every bar but to be added when you move to another section of the song. Likewise, the bongos make an interesting and musical topping but you wouldn't want them playing throughout a song.

Now look at the kick and snare in the two bars in Figure 5.24. Again, there's more variation in the kick and this time, in the first bar at least, the snare manages an extra hit. There are also two hi hat patterns here using both open and closed hats. Again, these can

M	Sound	Q	1			2			3			4		2		2		2		3			4	
	Bass Drum 1	16	◇					◇		◇	◇◇	◇◇◇◇						◇◇◇		◇		◇		
	Side Stick	16																						
	Ac. Snare	16			◇			◇◇						◇				◇					
	Hand Clap	16																						
	El. Snare	16																						
	LowFloorTom	16																						
	Cls HiHat	16	◇◇		◇		◇◇◇◇			◇		◇◇		◇		◇◇			◇◇◇◇					
	HiFloorTom	16																						
	Pedal HiHat	16																						
	Low Tom	16																						
	Open HiHat	16		◇			◇											◇					
	LowMid Tom	16																						

Figure 5.24: More Hip Hop variations.

be used in place of the straight eights when required.

You can funk up these patterns by adding additional snares and creating more complex plays between kick and snare.

And don't forget the scratch – it's an essential part of the Hip Hop sound! – although it's not something you'd use on every song. Most XG and GS drum sets have a scratch sound which you can drop into a song at suitable places.

Hip Hop bass

Hip Hop basses are generally simple but, of course, some songs have a bass line which uses more complex rhythms. We'll stick with simple. The top line in Figure 5.25 shows a dubby kind of bass rhythm which grooves along nicely. Below is a variation on it. See how you can play with these rhythms.These are essentially single-bar rhythms and the four bars we've shown assume that the chord sequence changes after two bars. If a chord sequence lasted for eight bars, you could play the same bar eight times.

Figure 5.25: A dubby Hip Hop bass and variation.

Figure 5.26 shows another two phrases. The first one contains another simple, single-bar phrase. The second example is a two-bar phrase but mainly because it plays other melody notes (the second bar rhythm is exactly the same as the first bar apart from a missing last note). Although not the same as the first example, you can see how it has borrowed aspects of the rhythm.

The patterns are all simple but effective.

Figure 5.26: Two more Hip Hop bass lines borrowing rhythms from the first example.

Trip Hop drums

Some say Trip Hop is Hip Hop slowed down and without the rap, and you can, indeed, create Trip Hop tracks from Hip Hop rhythms although you'd probably want to remove some of the hits. The overall feel is not quite as funky (or a loose, slow funk if you must) but it does have a groove and a psychedelic, trippy flavour.

Much use is made of echoes and spacey sounds, and consequently it's difficult to produce an authentic Trip Hop feel with a GM drum set – which is true of many forms of Dance music.

However, we can lay down the basics and if you apply a splash of reverb or a dark EQ to the kick or snare you'll be moving in the right direction. But samples are the way to go here.

Figure 5.27 shows two bars of Trip Hop patterns. You get the general groove from the kick and snare. In the first bar we've programmed the cabasa on the offbeat to produce a sort of swishy sound and you could use this on its own with the kick and snare. You could also program this line on hi hats, tambourine or any other sound which takes your fancy. The hi hat line here helps chug the rhythm along.

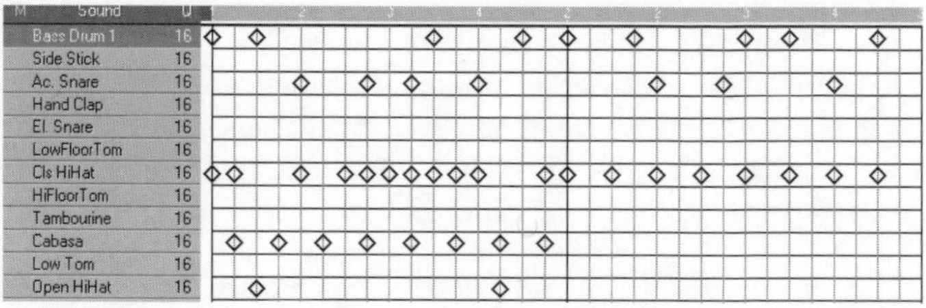

Figure 5.27: Two smooth Trip Hop bars and additional drum lines

In the second bar we have eighth hi hats on the beat just to show that they can work on or off the beat. You could throw in the odd open hi hat for variation.

Reggae drums

Trip Hop has roots in Reggae so in case you want to go back to the roots, here are some Reggae patterns. The emphasis in Reggae is very much on the offbeat, on beats two and four.

Figure 5.28 shows two Reggae variations. In both bars, the interplay is between the kick and snare but we've added a low tom in the second bar on the offbeat for emphasis. The hi hats tick away in fours or eights.

Bar one also includes a simple timbale pattern which you can dot around the drum track for variation. Bar two contains a pattern on cowbell and hi bongo (keep the velocity of these down so they don't overwhelm the main rhythm) and, as with many topping patterns in Dance, you can try these with different drum sounds.

M	Sound	Q															
	Bass Drum 1	16		◇			◇	◇		◇		◇		◇	◇◇		
	Side Stick	16															
	Ac. Snare	16	◇◇		◇		◇◇◇		◇		◇◇		◇◇	◇◇		◇◇	
	Hand Clap	16															
	El. Snare	16															
	LowFloorTom	16															
	Cls HiHat	16	◇	◇	◇	◇	◇	◇	◇	◇		◇		◇		◇	
	HiFloorTom	16															
	Tambourine	16															
	Low Tom	16									◇				◇		
	Open HiHat	16															
	LowMid Tom	16															
	HighTimbale	16	◇	◇			◇										
	LowTimbale	16				◇											
	Cowbell	16								◇	◇	◇	◇	◇	◇	◇	◇
	Hi Bongo	16								◇		◇		◇		◇	

Figure 5.28: Reggae patterns – at the root of Trip Hop.

Trip Hop bass

A Trip Hop bass line can draw on many influences from those in its roots all the way up to jazz. Generally, however, it's not too busy, serving to reinforce the chord structure and melody and leaving gaps for other instruments to move in and out. The dubby bass lines of Hip Hop and Drum & Bass (coming up next) work well (suitably adjusted for tempo, of course) although, depending on the music, you can engage in more strenuous bass activity if occasion demands.

In trippy mode it's not uncommon for a song to be built around just a couple of chords which makes it easy to improvise. Figure 5.29 demonstrates three Trip Hop basses, all two-bar patterns.

In the first pattern, notice how the rhythm of the notes follows the kick and snare pattern in our first Trip Hop drum rhythm. This

Figure 5.29: Three Trip Hop bass lines.

makes a really good groove, nice and tight (although that's not necessarily what you're looking for in a Trip Hop line).

The second example is somewhat minimal but it also emphasises the rhythm of the first three notes in the drum pattern. The third example is rather busier but, again, it follows the rhythms which we've used in the Trip Hop drum patterns.

In all cases, notice how the bass rhythms complement the drum rhythms, even if they don't play in perfect sync – and they don't have to. The simple melodies use only a few notes but fit well into the trippy mood. Without getting into music theory, this is mainly due to the Ab (G#) in the riffs which produce a tension when played against a Dm chord. You could improvise around these notes and rhythms for the best part of a song.

Jungle and Drum & Bass drums

Many original Jungle and Drum & Bass patterns were created by playing fast and loose with drum rhythms in a sampler and, as with Techno, the sound of the drums is very important. The result of the sample bending was low-pitched kick drums, and higher pitched snares and hi hats. We can program the pattern using a GM kit but sampled-based sounds will produce a more authentic feel.

Because the music rattles along at a fair pace, too many booming kicks would only serve to confuse, so many patterns simply have one kick at the start of the bar. On top of the kick we can play with snare rolls and hi hat patterns which are the essence of D&B. Another thing to note is that although the music may race along, there is often a half feel about it so it helps if you think in terms of two- and four-bar phrases rather than one-bar patterns.

The hi hat can actually sit on the offbeat throughout although you might like to juxtapose it with other drums or create individual patterns for it.

Figure 5.30 shows a two-bar pattern with hi hats on the offbeat and a sparse kick drum. But it's the snare rolls which make the pattern move. We've used the electric snare on the GM kit here which is closer to the D&B sound.

Figure 5.30: A two-bar Drum & Bass pattern with rolling snares.

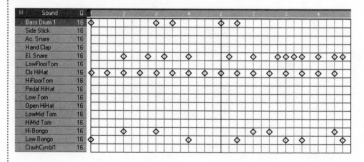

Notice the interplay between the kick and snare in the first bar, especially the little pattern they play around beat three. This is a common riff which could be used in the first beat of a bar (minus the leading snare hit, of course) or you could simply drop it in a song at various points for variety.

M	Sound	Q											
	Bass Drum 1	16											
	Side Stick	16											
	Ac. Snare	16											
	Hand Clap	16											
	El. Snare	16											
	LowFloorTom	16											
	Cls HiHat	16											
	HiFloorTom	16											
	Pedal HiHat	16											
	Low Tom	16											
	Open HiHat	16											
	LowMid Tom	16											

Figure 5.31 More Drum & Bass variations.

There's also a bongo pattern here which could be played on congas or other drums or sounds. This doesn't want to dominate the rhythm so don't set the velocities too high.

Figure 5.31 shows another variation with a bare kick drum, and a closed hi hat now shares the job with an open hi hat. And still the snares roll. As ever, vary the snare velocities.

It's easy to construct snare patterns using a drum or grid editor. Draw a row of snare hits onto the grid, play back the pattern and then remove one or two at a time. Listen to the pattern. Sometimes it won't sound so good so put the hits back and remove other ones.

Drum & Bass also makes good use of snare rolls and here you can try 1/16th and even 1/32nd note rolls. Kick drum rolls are also common so substitute the kick for the snare.

You may also hear the roll increasing in pitch as it nears the end of its run. This is difficult to do with MIDI as you need to gradually pitch shift the sound. However, some audio editors such as Cool Edit 2000 can vary the shift over the length of a file which is exactly what we want to do. You need to record the roll as an audio file, process it and import it into your sequencer.

The bass in Jungle and Drum & Bass

We said that Drum & Bass often has a half feel and the bass line can contribute to this by playing few notes, leaving gaps and spreading phrases over four bars. We're talking simple here.

Figure 5.32 shows the sort of thing; an eight-bar phrase with few notes. Notice that the second note (the C) in the first three groups is syncopated and plays slightly before the third beat. This helps drive the music along. However, it could actually be played on the third beat. It could also be pulled forwards and played on the second beat.

Figure 5.32: A dubby Drum & Bass bass line.

Figure 5.33: Variations on the simple Drum & Bass bass line.

Figure 5.34: Two slightly more complex Drum & Bass bass lines.

Sine waves

A sine wave is a pure sound containing no harmonics other than its fundamental frequency from which we get the pitch of the note. You'll find sine waves on all synthesisers.

Both these variations are shown in Figure 5.33.

Figure 5.34 shows two more four-bar phrases which are still fairly simple. Notice the gaps. Don't be afraid to leave an empty bar.

Of course, bass lines can be more complex and, as ever, it depends on the underlying drum patterns and the music. The bass sounds are very important, too. Try a low pitched, sub-bass sound, almost like a sine wave – but watch those speakers!

Grooves and quantisation

Of necessity, we've used a drum grid editor to illustrate the drum patterns, and notation for the bass lines. However, all Dance music is about hitting the groove and when creating songs you will often want to humanise a part. We touched upon this briefly when we suggested randomising velocity levels to remove the machine gun effect of a row of hi hats played quickly in succession.

Many sequencers go a step beyond this with a groove function. Quantisation was developed to push and pull notes onto certain divisions of the beat. It's but a small step to produce groove templates which place notes onto pre-programmed and user-defined beat divisions rather than the 'on the beat' divisions used by standard quantisation.

Emagic's Logic includes a set of grooves and Cubase VST has a Groove Control function, Figure 5.35, where grooves can be selected and tweaked. Using a function like this can quickly give a part more life and remove the mechanicalness which clicking notes into an editor can often produce.

Drum tricks – new parts for old

Here's a trick for producing new drum parts.

As you probably know, each drum in a MIDI drum voice responds to a different MIDI note number. MIDI note 36 (C1) triggers

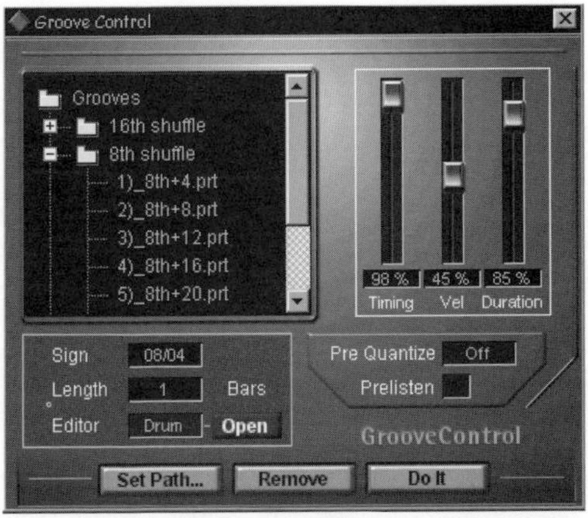

Figure 5.35: VST's Groove Control makes it easy to adjust the feel of a pattern

a kick drum, 38 plays a snare, 39 is a hand clap and so on. If we transpose a drum part, the kick could end up being played on castanets so the last thing we want to do is transpose a drum part, right? Wrong!

By playing a rhythm on a different set of drums you may be surprised how many good sounds and rhythms you hear. Transposing drums can be an excellent way of leveraging your patterns in the search for something new and different.

You can transpose the entire pattern simply by transposing the track it's on. However, an even better way to use transpose is to put each drum on its own track as described at the beginning of the chapter. Set the pattern to play back in a loop and then transpose each of the drums one at a time. This way you can keep the essential kick and snare drums (or whatever drums you deem essential) and experiment with the toppings. Or even look for alternatives to the kick and snare.

Would this line be better on hi or low tom, or conga or agogo? Questions like these are easily and quickly answered. Keep the list of the drums and their MIDI note numbers handy; they should be listed in the instrument's documentation.

Sample editing, processing and manipulation

hen working with samples and sample loops, there are two basic functions you will inevitably need to do. The first is to trim a sample so there is no gap or silence at the beginning or end, and the second is to create a loop. To do these things you need an audio editor.

Most sound cards and several sample-based sequencing programs include an audio editor and these are fine for trimming samples. However, making loops is not quite as straightforward and you really need the assistance of some software. We'll get to that in a moment.

Trimming samples

When you trigger a sample, the last thing you want is a short gap before it kicks in. In some sequencing software, you can mask the start and end of a sample so only a selected portion of it plays. This can be used to play, say, just one part of a sample which contains two or more hits or sounds, Figure 6.1, and it's very useful.

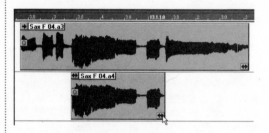

Figure 6.1: In Cubase you can determine which section of a sample will play.

It could also be used to mask gaps at the start and end of a sample but that's really a bit of a kludge. It's not very elegant, you have to do it each time you use the sample, the 'silence' uses disk space, and you can't successfully use the sample in a program which does not have the mask feature. Do the decent thing and cut it out.

Trimming is easy. The main thing to remember is to zoom in on the start and end so you can see exactly where you're cutting. Figure 6.2, shows a drum sound in Cool Edit 2000 with some silence or noise at the beginning. We've highlighted the section where the drum starts because Cool Edit has a Zoom To Selection feature. With other editors you may simply click on a Zoom button. If we zoom in close we can see exactly where the drum sound begins, Figure 6.3, and it's then an easy matter to select the leading section and remove it.

Repeat the process at the end of the sample but beware of chopping out the tail. Drum sounds such as cymbals tend to 'ring on' at the end and it's easy to remove this if you're not careful. After marking the end of a tail, select the remaining sample and listen to

The size of silence

....

All digital audio files recorded at the same sample rate and resolution and of the same duration are the same size and take up the same physical space on your hard disk. It doesn't make any difference whether the file contains a recording of a classical symphony or complete and utter silence.

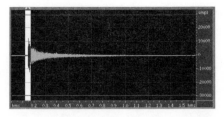 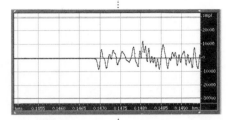

it. Most editors have an option for playing the selected portion of a file. When you're happy with what you hear, then cut.

Figure 6.2 (left): A drum sample with unwanted noise at the beginning.

Going loopy

Many audio editors have features to help you make good loops. What you're trying to do is to match the end of a wave with its start so it flows back to the beginning without a click or breaking the beat. Easier said than done.

The first step is to load the sample and select what you think are good start and end points. Many programs will play this back while you adjust them so you can hear what the loop sounds like. Some also provide a visual display showing how the end of the sample leads into the start of it. Steinberg's WaveLab does this and Figure 6.4 shows that the end and start of the sample do not match up at all, which will create a click on looping.

Figure 6.3 (right): Zooming in makes it easy to see where the drum sound actually begins.

Before you trim...
....

Before performing any edit function on a sample *make a backup.*

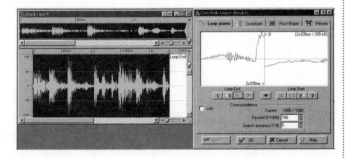

Figure 6.4: The end and start points of the loop don't match up at all.

You can nudge the start and end points manually but the program also has a pattern-matching algorithm which helps find good loop points such as that in Figure 6.5 where the points flow together better.

Making better loops

If you're recording sounds for looping, record them twice in succession and use the second one for the loop. This applies particularly to sounds which have a tail or some reverb at the end.

Figure 6.5: WaveLab has selected better end and start points for the loop but you must listen to it before believing it.

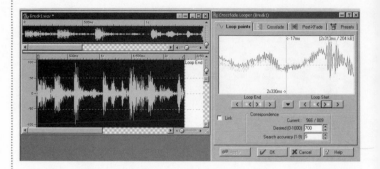

The reason is this. If the sound is looped, the tail part will be cut off each time it starts a new cycle because it wasn't present at the beginning of the recording. If you loop the second take, the tail will be present at the beginning of the loop. Looping the first take in such a case can make the loop sound unnatural.

Crossfade

Crossfading is a process which fades out one sample while fading in another – just like fading between two records but on a smaller scale.

Stubborn loop tip

If you have a loop which simply won't – here's a tip to help make it! Crossfade the start of the loop with the end.

Copy a section from the start of the file and mix it with the section at the end of the file. Most editors have a Paste Mix function or something similar to allow you to do this. Ideally, you want to crossfade the mix so the sound is introduced gradually. You will doubtless have to experiment with the size of the section to copy from and mix to.

WaveLab has a facility for doing this almost automatically, plus a neat tool for the most stubborn of all stubborn loops. It's the Wave Equaliser which evens out changes in volume and tone and crossfades the end and start, too.

Heading for a crash

The best reverse cymbal effects come from crash cymbals, preferably one with a long tail. But do try ride cymbals and other drum sounds, too.

The old reverse cymbal trick

All but the most basic of audio editors have a wealth of functions useful to the Dance musician. Check out the reverse function which simply reverses a sample so it plays backwards. Cymbals are everyone's favourite reverse sample and this can be used at the start of a song (a bit hackneyed now) or to lead into a new section (still hackneyed but still effective).

Position the sample so the end of it, where the reverse cymbal reaches its crescendo, coincides with the first beat of the section it's leading into. This is easy to do in a MIDI/audio sequencer. If it has a function which snaps parts to the nearest bar you will probably have to switch this off.

Experiments in pitch and time

Many types of Dance use samples whose pitch or tempo has been radically altered. Most audio editors have time stretch and pitch shift functions which do this. Normally, changing the pitch of a sample will also change its duration as we discussed in Chapter 4. Sometimes these two functions are combined which makes it easier to apply one without the side effect of the other, or to apply both functions together.

There is a vast range of possibilities here such as increasing the tempo of a slow Dance loop up to Jungle speed, pitching up a drum part to Acid levels or lowering it for a Trip Hop loop.

When messing with pitch and time, check if the function has a formants control. This may simply preserve the formants or it may let you change them. If it preserves them you can safely pitch vocals up and down. If you can change them you can transform a voice from male to female or vice versa or even have a stab at an androgynous vox.

Creative formant control can change the characteristics of any sound and it's well worth experimenting with this if you're looking to change the tone of a sound before turning to the EQ section.

Also, as briefly mentioned in Chapter 5 in the Jungle and Drum & Bass drums section, some editors can vary the change as the file progresses – creating a sound which gradually changes in pitch or tempo. This is a superb feature to apply not only to drum rolls but to individual drum samples (particularly ethnic drums) and it's great for special FX, too.

Reality distortion

Noise and dirt – the audio sort – play a major part in the samples used in genres such as Hardcore, Gabba and Tech Step. Some thoughtful editors such as Cool Edit even have a built-in distortion function, Figure 6.6 with controllable parameters.

If your editor doesn't have a distortion function, a sample can be distorted in several other ways. You can reduce the sample rate or resolution. This has the effect of reducing the higher harmonics and making the sound grungy.

You can amplify the wave several times so the top and bottom are clipped, Figure 6.7. This is a real distorted sound. The more you amplify, the more noisy and distorted it becomes.

Other tricks include severe filtering to remove or severely reduce particular frequency bands. You could filter the low frequency kick drum from a loop, or the hi hats – or the sounds in the middle of the frequency band. Or boost these frequencies into distortion.

If the editor has a dynamics section, severe compression may

Formant informant

Formants are the resonant frequencies created by the shape and size of a sound source such as the voice box, a guitar, a string or brass instrument and which are responsible for its tonal characteristics. It's what makes a male voice sound masculine and a female voice sound feminine. Transposing a voice upwards without preserving the formants produces what is known as the 'chipmunk' effect.

Dynamo dynamics

Dynamics processing is used to change the dynamic range of a signal which is the difference in volume between the quietest and loudest sections. It's traditionally used to 'even out' these ups and down so the total sound plays at a more even volume level.

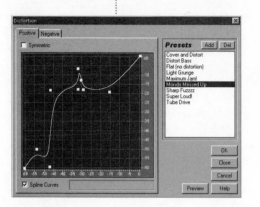

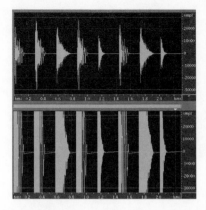

Figure 6.6 (left): Cool Edit's Distortion function can make even the sweetest sound into something decidedly worse!

Figure 6.7 (right): Severely increasing the amplitude of the top waveform causes the edges to clip as in the lower example.

produce distortion or a pumping effect. Even effects such as reverb, echo and flanging can distort a sound if driven to extremes.

Plug-in effects

If you really want to marmalise a sample and take it to hell and back, you may need something a little more than the processes built into the average editor. Enter plug-ins. There are hundreds of these, many of them are free on the Web or else cost very little. Check out The DirectX Files web site which is listed in the Appendix.

Plug-ins provide many processes which may not be found in an editor as well as offering high quality effects for those who need them. In the processing line, Steinberg's GRM Tools is one of the most interesting.

Specially developed for sound designers, it contains an extreme set of tools for applying the most radical filtering processing to a sample, combined with sample slicers, transposers and harmonic manipulators. The effects can all be applied dynamically in real-time so the sound evolves during production.

ReCycling loops

One of the most interesting things you can do to loops is split them up and put them together again in a different order. Or perhaps you'd like to substitute one sample in the loop for another. Trying to do this manually is near impossible but Steinberg's ReCycle was designed to do just that.

It finds the hits in a loop, effectively dividing it into its component parts, then it saves each part as a separate sample. Now, if you load the samples one after the other into a sequencer it will play the original loop. However, because the samples are separate you can process them individually, pan them individually, substitute one sample for another or import a sample of your own to take its place. All the while, the original groove is preserved.

What's more, because the loop has been split into its component parts, if you change the tempo of the sequencer, the samples will be played back faster or slower so the tempo of the loop will change without any change in pitch.

New loops from old

Another excellent loop manipulation tool is Button Production's Zero-X BeatCreator. This also slices up loops but then allows you to shuffle the bits around to come up with new loops. If you can't be bothered to do that it'll do if for you. It can also apply different types of EQ to selected sections. The result is totally new loops from your existing material in seconds. It can reverse sections, it can do time stretch, change the pitch, it has distortion, and it has a neat function to detect the pitch of a section. Contact details are in the Appendix.

Processing MIDI recordings

MIDI recordings offer ultimate control over tempo and every single drum hit, and it's very easy to experiment with the rhythm. But you can't do the neat processing stuff that you can with samples, can you? Oh yes you can! But you need to convert your MIDI files into audio first.

This is usually very easy. Many sound cards have an internal connection which lets you select their MIDI output as the recording source, much as you can select their Mic or line input. Select it, fire up your sequencer, start playback and record the output onto a spare audio track. If your card doesn't have this feature you can simply connect the sound card's audio output to its audio input and record the MIDI playback that way.

Special mention must be made of Yamaha's SW1000XG card and accompanying XGWorks software which has a built-in function for recording MIDI parts as audio. It makes it very easy.

So, once you've recorded your MIDI parts, trim them and process them.

7

Putting your music on the Web

After all the hard work you've put into creating your own Dance music, you'll want a wider audience to hear it. And you can do just that by putting your music on the Web.

You can design your own Web site and upload your music there for people to listen to and download but that's a lot of hard work and it's not easy making people aware of your Web site or persuading them to visit unless you're already a known artist with a following. However, as you write more music, having your own Web site is a good idea so keep this one on the back burner.

The easiest way to promote your music on the Web is via one of the numerous 'music community' sites which are springing up. They feature music by up and coming musicians and occasionally feature tracks by well-known artists.

Mixing with the best

If you are using proprietary Dance music software such as Mixman or eJay check the developers' Web pages first, because some have a community area where users can upload their music for visitors to listen to and download. You may also find new samples, tutorials, and hints and tips on using the software here, too.

Music communities

If you use other software and can save your music in an audio format, you should look at the music community sites. We list a few here but more are springing up all the time:

www.peoplesound.com
www.besonic.com
www.mp3.com
www.getoutthere.bt.com
www.vitaminic.com

These sites contains thousands of pieces of music covering a wide range of styles so you can hear what other people have been creating and see how popular various tracks have been.

Different sites offer different facilities. For example, in some cases you receive a fee when people download your music and although this is quite modest, some of the top-selling artists on these sites have made thousands in royalties. Some sites allow you to set up a web page and promote your music for free. Others will produce a CD, sell it for you and give you a royalty for each one sold (usually a goodly proportion of the sale price).

How to get more downloads

If you're using a site which pays according to how many times your music is downloaded, here's a tip to help you get more downloads – keep the size of your music files short!

Yes, it's got nothing to do with the quality of the music but the fact is, most people are still logging onto the Net with 56K modems at best and they're much more likely to download a song file which is 2.2Mb in size than 8.2Mb. That's not always the case, of course, but check the size of the song files in the site's Top 20 and see how well this theory holds...

Of course, having a good music track helps, too, because visitors can preview the music before they download it.

What audio format?

If you're working with audio on the PC you'll be using Wave files. On the Mac they will probably be AIFF files. These are uncompressed audio files formats and a five-minute song in stereo will have a file size of around 50Mb. That's far too large for most folks to download until we're all equipped with hi speed digital connections, so all music sites use a compressed audio format which reduces the file size by a factor of 10 to 12 or more. These are all lossy compression systems although they claim 'CD quality' (and many people can't tell the difference), and you should always keep a copy of your music in native Wave or AIFF format.

There are several compressed audio formats but far and away the most popular, currently at least, is MP3. This offers compression ratios of up to 80:1 although there is a trade off between file size and quality. In practice, compression ratios of around 10 or 12 are used which results in good quality audio and manageable file sizes.

Lossy compression

As it says, this form of compression reduces a file by discarding information which most people's ears won't miss. The algorithms can be quite complex but a file may lose some low frequency content, for example. and some stereo information.

Saving your music as MP3

Wave and AIFF files are easily converted to MP3 format but, of course, you need software to do the job. Many audio editors can do it including WaveLab and Cool Edit 2000. There are stand-alone commercial programs such as Cakewalk's Pyro and Magix's MP3 Maker, and there are the inevitable free programs on the Web. Check out MusicMatch Jukebox, Xing Technology's AudioCatalyst and CDex to name but three (Web site details are in the Appendix).

MP3

MP3 stands for MPEG 1 Audio Layer 3 and MPEG stands for the Moving Picture Experts Group which gave its name to several audio and video file formats.

Other audio formats

There are other formats out there which claim to compress a file to an even smaller size yet retain more audio quality. However, the big battle is not so much with compression and quality but with the ability to restrict distribution. MP3 files can be sent to anyone, freely copied and played on dozens of MP3 players. The new technologies are geared towards the requirements of record companies who want to sell music, not give it away.

There may be a shift away from MP3 but what will take its place is anyone's guess. With so many people having invested in pocket-sized MP3 players it's unlikely that MP3 will lie down and die in the near future, and in any event, it many still continue to be the format of choice for people who want their music freely copied and distributed.

Watch the music web sites which, obviously, keep an eye on new developments. When they start supporting other formats you'll know the tide is turning.

Other audio formats include Beatnik and Yamaha's Sound VQ which both have pros and cons. However, the one with the biggest company behind it is undoubtedly Microsoft's WMA (Windows Media Audio) which has provision for copy protection and which also boasts good audio quality and compression.

T he Web is crawling with resources for the Dance musician – everything from freeware and shareware to demos of commercial software so you can try before you buy. But it's main value lies in its superabundance of samples, loops, and songs in every conceivable musical genre you can think of. Much of this is totally free although there are squillions of sample CDs for sale out there, too.

Appendix

Books

It's with a noticeable amount of self-effacement that we recommend these books to you as they all come from the same publisher that brings you this fine book. PC Publishing is a specialist in the field and just happens to publish a range of books which are dedicated to hi tech music.

Quick Guide to MP3 and Digital Music
Quick Guide to Analogue Synthesis
Quick Guide to Digital Audio Recording
Advanced MIDI User's Guide
Cubase VST Tips and Tricks
Fast Guide to Cubase VST
Fast Guide to Emagic Logic
Handbook of MIDI Sequencing
Making Music with Emagic Logic Audio
PC Music The Easy Guide

You can get more details at www.pc-publishing.co.uk and place an order on-line.
Tel: +44 (0) 1732 770893
Fax: +44 (0) 1732 770268

Web sites

Aludra	www.aludra.com	Beat 2000
Best Service	www.bestservice.de	Media DJ Pro, ReLoop, Sound Engine Plus
Bias	www.bias-inc.com	Peak audio editor for the Mac
BitHeadz	www.bitheadz.com	Phrazer, software synths, samplers and drum machines
Button Prodns	www.beatcreator.com	BeatCreator sample slicer and loop creator
Cakewalk	www.cakewalk.com	Cakewalk sequencers

CDex	www.cdex.n3.net	CDex CD audio extractor and MP3 encoder software
Data Becker	www.databecker.com	DJ 2000
Emagic	www.emagic.de	Logic Audio sequencers
FastTrak	www.fasttrak.com, www.ejay.com	Dance eJay series
Fruity Loops	www.fruityloops.com	Fruity Loops
fxpansion	www.fxpansion.com	Drum sample players and VST plug-ins
IK Multimedia	www.groovemaker.com	GrooveMaker
Keyfax	www.keyfax.com	PhatBoy MIDI controller and MIDI drum patterns
Magix	www.magix.com	Magix range of music software
Mixman	www.mixman.com	Mixman Studio
MusicMatch	www.musicmatch.com	MusicMatch Jukebox MP3 player and encoder
Modified	www.modified.com	Chillas, frEQency 99
Making Waves	www.makingwavesaudio.co.uk	Making Waves
Propellerhead	www.propellerheads.de	ReBirth
Shareware Music Machine	www.sharewaremusicmachine.com	Lots of music shareware programs
Softkey	www.softkey.co.uk	Pro DJ
Sonic Foundry	www.sonicfoundry.com	Acid and Sound Forge audio editor
soundfonts.com	www.soundfonts.com	Everything you ever wanted to know about SoundFonts, plus links and samples
Steinberg	www.steinberg.net	Cubase VST sequencers, WaveLab audio editor, plug-ins
Synthzone	www.synthzone.com	Loads of info on synths and drums and links to sample and MIDI file sites
Syntrillium	www.syntrillium.com	Cool Edit 2000 audio editor
TC Works	www.tcworks.de	Spark audio editor for the Mac
Techland	www.techlandsoft.com	Future Beat 3D
The DirectX Files	www.thedirectxfiles.com	Super source of plug-ins info
Time + Space	www.timespace.com	Sample CD distributor
Yamaha	www.yamaha.co.uk	Sound cards, MIDI modules, musical instruments
Xing Technology	www.xingtech.com	AudioCatalyst MP3 software

Dance music Web resources

Danceportal	www.danceportal.co.uk	Events, reviews, features, links
Vagabondage	www.vagabondage.com/genres/	Generates 1645 variations on Dance music sub-genre names
Dance music resource pages	www.juno.co.uk	New UK Dance releases and imports plus sound clips and track listings
Intelligent Dance Music	www.hyperreal.org/music/lists/idm/	A mailing list for the discussion of the Intelligent Dance Music subset of electronic music
DJ Rhythms Dance music database	www.djrhythms.com/db/	A discographical catalogue tabulating a partial history of Dance music releases, mainly House and Techno

Index